GOING
OUT OF BUSINESS
BY DESIGN

Why Seventy Percent of Small Businesses Fail

GOING
OUT OF BUSINESS
BY DESIGN

Why Seventy Percent of Small Businesses Fail

TOM PEASE

New York

Going Out of Business By Design
Why Seventy Percent of Small Business Fail

ISBN 978-1-60037-671-9 (pbk)
ISBN 978-1-60037-672-6 (hc)

Library of Congress Control Number: 2009930205

MORGAN · JAMES
THE ENTREPRENEURIAL PUBLISHER

Morgan James Publishing, LLC
1225 Franklin Ave., STE 325
Garden City, NY 11530-1693
Toll Free 800-485-4943
www.MorganJamesPublishing.com

In an effort to support local communities, raise awareness and funds, Morgan James Publishing donates one percent of all book sales for the life of each book to Habitat for Humanity. Get involved today, visit www.HelpHabitatForHumanity.org.

DEDICATIONS

It is truly a pleasure to have this book in print. It has been written by many people who have lived the story and the lessons in it from the past 29 years. These are the people who have kept me from going out of business by design. It might take a while.

I thank first, the **Good Lord,** for keeping me healthy, productive, and in the game this far.

My wife **Cindy** for enduring all, for fearlessly signing all co-signs, and for saying she never worried about any of them. Prayer warrior. Smart. I would have been wayward somewhere by now without her.

My mother Josephine (in memoriam) who instilled values, especially moral and spiritual ones, and those concerning the ills that befall us, that tell me what I need to be to be a good employer, a good person.

My father **Tom,** 85, who bequeaths mental toughness, discipline, and businessman's blood. Charter member of Greatest Generation. Soldier. Bronze Star, two Purple Hearts. Stalwart Christian. Iron Man. Platinum Peddler. Made of Wow Stuff.

Hero to his family. As father of eight Dad ran a small business before going out the door in the morning.

To all employees and former employees, especially **Mark Stevens**, here from day one. To **Theo Harris** for his 25 years of trust. To **Cindy McLarty,** VP and CFO, who brought needed accounting and administrative skills, neither of which I had. For sharing the mental responsibilities with me and trying to ease them with her positive thinking and generous demeanor. To **Debe Webster,** my assistant in everything, who possesses more blades than any Swiss Army knife. To **Linda Camp,** for undeterred friendship, humor, and sales making. To my son **Parker,** who had the courage and faith to cast his business career with his father. For being his own person, just like I would. For putting in five years at the University of Memphis. To **Paul Ginn,** a person I admire.

To Cliff Conner, (in memoriam), my earliest banker, who taught me a lot.

To **Ed Neal,** my 29 year CPA who taught me how to understand those dials on the dashboard as well as on the financial statements.

To **Della Grant**, the only business partner I ever chose, and my friend for 29 years.

To **Jim Cross,** my leasing agent since the beginning, who has helped me finance many things, especially when they had to get a little creative.

To **Rob Hale,** my attorney, who has always gotten me a great outcome in serious matters.

To **Mary Singer,** the world's greatest tenant representative.

To **Lacey,** my daughter, who worked for me a brief time and candidly told me she did not like it. For the just plain joy of you. Thank you for encouraging me to 'write my story.'

TABLE OF CONTENTS

PREFACE

"Two roads diverged in a wood, and I took the one
Less traveled and that has made all the difference."
Robert Frost

This famous line from a simple poem tells it. What road are you taking as an OE--owner/entrepreneur? What design? What strategy? Do you have one? Your choices make all the difference. "By design" I mean the philosophy, execution and principle behind your decision making. This includes pricing, selling, HR, financing, marketing and how you lead. It is your creation, your design—beautiful or not so.

Early in my career I was frustrated by a competitor selling our brand for a much lower price. After paying a salesman and all expenses, I just did not see how he could do it. I asked the manufacturer if he was getting a lower price. No, we had the same. "So how can he do this Larry?" "He can't Tom. Not for long. This is called going out of business by design." This phrase stuck.

Bad design is plentiful in small business and can be heard in typical comments from OEs: "Just get the business". "We want to be number one". "If I sell enough I will win a trip". "Go as low as you need to win ". "I haven't raised my prices in years". "I haven't got time for their personal problems". "I never did understand all that ratio mumbo jumbo." "Salespeople are overpaid." "There is nothing you can do about it." "I don't want to fool with all that new tech stuff." "It's what my uncle always said to do."

Owning a business still seems to be one of the those American Dreams and it can indeed be so. But more often, as the failure statistics show, it turns into a nightmare. Some of this is preventable with good business design and discipline.

OE's go into business, get going, but still are ignorant about what sustains a business. Within those areas of design ignorance lie their demise. It may not be too different from a pilot who knows how to take off, but not stay airborne! Why bother to take off to begin with? Some 70% of us are crashing! Makes no sense, right? The OE knows passion, product and what he wants to achieve. There are no shortages of people with these, but there are those who can channel that into a successful business. Surprisingly, or maybe not so, this is true for those in business some years too. The Small Business Administration says **56% of businesses do not make it past four years and 69% more than seven years**. In 2008, according to the *Wall Street Journal,* 64,000 businesses of all sizes went out of business. Probably one near you. Business bankruptcy filings are up 121% over 2006 according to Forbes. These are serious numbers and should warn OE's to be ever more diligent in their decision making. Hopefully, this book can help with that.

What is going on here? Why do small businesses fail at such an alarmingly high rate? Often, the answer is the OE has, probably unknowingly, set in motion bad business designs that lead to business failure. Or, he has based important decisions on a flimsy, uninformed thought process. These are fundamental flaws that, like slow moving unchecked malignancies, eventually ruin good people and businesses, as statistics well attest. The good news is that the end takes a while, so there is time to make needed changes.

This book will try to alert you to them! These chapters will try to imbed in you blinking caution lights that go off when you enter any of the GOOB zones. It will point your thinking in the direction of fertile soil. It will try to beef up your thought muscles! My experiences take place within an office equipment business, e/Doc Systems, of 30 some employees, with gross profit of about 2 million dollars. I have owned it for 29 years.

To design means to draw up a plan. The OE has to be an architect and select the best elements for a good looking, long lasting, functional business. It takes more than one might think and the design changes over time. It needs to be continually modified, but in the right way. It cannot be done by just one person either. It takes professionals, such as CPA's, bankers, lawyers, advisors, and knowledgeable employees to get it right.

Entrepreneurs get lathered with ideas, get money, buy product and declare "I am going for it". That may be the high point. There is little preparation and littler understanding of, say, how to read a financial statement or ensure positive cash flow. A business instructor of mine had a name for this: TENE. This stood for Temporary Entrepreneurial Neuron Explosion-- the "big bang" theory of his business creation-- the creation he sees in his mind. When under this influence the OE feels the Great Inspiration and the rest should take care of itself. But life is daily in business ownership. So the OE needs to remember, he is not God and his creation is going to take a lot longer than seven days.

Enthusiasm, necessary as it is, won't put a nickel in an empty checkbook. Simple accounting terms such as hurdle rate, burden rate, gross margin, inventory turns, current ratio, are foreign to new owners. This can go for experienced owners as well. The astronomical failure rates of small businesses show how widespread bad design is.

With the exception of chapter one, this book is aimed at businesses under 50 employees-- about 90% of all businesses. It should be helpful to any business owner, but it assumes you have some staff. I don't know about you, but I do not want to hear another story about how great Steve Jobs, Bill Gates, Michael Dell are. There is nothing small about these guys! They run some of the biggest businesses in America. We don't. I do not write about anything unique to a manufacturing business, because I do not know anything about one. Lines in bold are meant to be highly significant. Lines with highlight are "planks" that make up essentials in good business design. We will compile these at the end of the book to compose our Best Business Design.

A business drawn up with incomplete or bad designs, which is the majority, will not stand the test of time. They will "blow down" in a good wind, which is the fate of 70% within seven years. *This is a lot of carnage and money lost.* Unfortunately, it also answers the question "How do you end up with a small fortune owning a business? Start with a large one." The 70% failure figure is comprehensive, meaning it includes every business from an upstart wig shop to a sophisticated Silicon Valley tech business.

This book may be more timely than originally thought with our 2009 economy, shedding jobs and businesses at twice the normal rate. This will mean more startup businesses will form, as people seek control over their own fate. It also means existing small businesses are more stressed than usual.

This is not a "How to Start a Business" book. A book will not start a business any more than reading one will get you married. Since 56% of start ups do not last four years, it bears mentioning, that whatever is being written in these start up books could stand re-evaluation. But if you are already committed and running, *Going Out of Business By Design* can help you. Its mission is to give helpful, real world information, that can prevent some problems from happening. It might give you or your managers a better way to think. It will show how to operate with good design elements and identify bad ones, that may take you out of business and prevent the personal and professional trauma that goes with it.

If you scan business books for sale, the majority seem to be trying to help you start a business. Fine. Most are of fluffy subject matter about how to get the right business structure, pay various taxes, set up a website, compile a spreadsheet, talk to a banker and other soft matter available anywhere. There are too few about how to correct your course, manage all the troubles, or think about things in a profitable manner for businesses already in the war zone. Hopefully, *Going Out Of Business By Design* is better.

Here's to reducing the 70%!

Note: I use the abbreviation GOOB to mean *going out of business by design.*

So as not to offend the female business owners I apologize in advance for using the pronoun "he" but constant he/she is cumbersome.

PART ONE:
Dealing With Yourself

Some days you are the pigeon and some days you are the statue. On the days you are the pigeon remember that you are always capable of flying high and leaping tall buildings in a single flight. On the days you are the statue let that remind you things can change at any moment.

In Part One you will learn that you are your biggest competitor, that the thought process (or lack of one) behind your decision making can be the difference between prospering or breaking the piggy bank wide open. There are things you must know in the financial, legal and management areas. Do you know the benchmarks for your industry, for example? Do you know pertinent financial ratios? Do you possess the needed leadership qualities to head a group of business people?

You are the most important asset your business has. Part One is all about you, taking care of you, and making sure you are up to the task of running a small business successfully.

Am I Right for This?

Yes, if you know all the
blades of a swiss army knife

I spoke at the local university after winning the Memphis Business Journal's Small Business Executive of the Year. The professor asked me to speak on how to decide if business ownership is right for an individual and what it took. My topic was "Should You Be Doing This At All". It is an important question considering the high failure rates of small businesses. Using the points of that talk we can surmise if it is good design for you to become an OE-- or continue to be one.

One of the simplest explanations for some business failures is that the person should never have taken the business ownership route in the first place. It just did not match up with their personal traits, skills or experience. This is having the benefit of hindsight. Then there is the counter to that which goes "well, you never know until you try." Admirable enough.

Nothing wrong with trying but let us make it one, very calculated, disciplined effort, so we do not end up being a statistic.

Many of the 70% failures are the equivalent of drunken sailors. Personal shortcomings are trying to be satisfied drinking in business ownership. Unfulfilled control freaks want business ownership. Sour grapes people wanting at ex-employers want business ownership. Ego types looking for a stage want business ownership. Bored types want business ownership. Too many people getting into business ownership for the wrong reasons and not enough for the right reasons, which are to be a professional businessperson and feed your passion. When the 'misguided' attitudes come to dominate the operation, then this is trouble.

Will you hang out a shingle as Dr. Jones (thankfully laws prevent this, but the 70% failure rate in business calls for a similar law) if you are not a doctor? Will you relish trying to heal people you do not know how to heal? Will you fly a plane without knowing the instruments? It is much the same with the would be entrepreneur, who is really not one. The statistics cry out for certification, before a person can claim to be a businessperson open for business.

The consequences of business failure (the 70% before seven years), with all its damages, justifies licensing for a business owner before claiming to be such. Can you read a financial statement? Can you sell? Do you have any credit? Can you lead? Can you compute your working capital position? Are you fit? Do you know what positive cash flow is? Can you handle adversity? Do you know your ratios and how to use technology? Etc. Much of this is like asking Michelangelo, if he knows how to work with stone. You would assume so. If not, then what are we doing here?

It might seem obvious, that people go into business to become good businesspersons and are reasonably versed in it. The statistics show this is not the case! I do not think there would be near the business failures, and all the expensive consequences of such for employees, owners, customers, and vendors alike, if so. What is really going on needs a sober assessment of the motives of a potential OE. Here is what I spoke at the University of Memphis on the needed disposition of one setting out on entrepreneurialism.

- It be worked into methodically. The decision should be an evolution more than a revolution. Build up job related experience. Learn all you can where you work. Attend seminars. Talk to professionals in other disciplines such as finance. Read books. Talk with those doing it. Do homework. If you rush in, you will probably rush out too.

- Stick with what you know. If you have been working in the technology field, it would not be promising to go into, say, owning a restaurant. Much of your experience will go to waste. Your chances for failure will increase. Learning general business is important, but then learning a particular industry is, as well. If you already know one, then that is your best chance.

- Sales experience is best training. Sales work comes closest to duplicating ownership demands. Starting at zero each month, as well as meeting a yearly goal, is what an owner experiences.

- Be guided by your predominant trait. Are you fiercely independent or a consensus builder? Are you highly creative or a stickler of detail? Are you an introvert or extrovert? Make sure the business you start suits your personality. If you are predominately a creative person, it may not make sense to open an accounting franchise. Independent types will not do well with partners. It is essential that your personality traits are compatible with the particular demands for successful operation for your type business. A mismatch here is a death sentence or misery, at the least.

- It is harder to keep a business going, than get it going. Good to keep in mind the failure stats on this one.

Keeping it going requires other skills than the ones to get it going. This whole book is really about how to keep things going. Do you know how to borrow money? Have you hired people that can sustain you? Is your own energy keeping up? Have you hired people that know?

- <u>You must be a good manager and recruiter of people.</u> The CEO's main job is to manage capital, the green kind and the human kind. It is a moving target, like shoveling smoke. If you are not good at it best to stay very small. Hire expertise you do not have. Key on energy. The better recruiter you are the greater your chances for avoiding failure. Remember that management means getting things done through other people. If you are always doing it, you have made recruiting mistakes.

- <u>Best to have a business that starts other ones.</u> Sell products that yield service revenue and supply revenue. Products that "eat and drink". The razor sale generates a lifetime of shaving cream revenue. Straight retail product is riskiest. Success in retail needs a good economy and that is not always the case. Your business model should have a good chunk of revenue in service and supply revenue to be successful.

- <u>Buy one instead of start one.</u> This may be a good idea if you are not the start up kind of person, but have the rest of your house in order. Owner financing is usually a big part of a purchase. Step right in! Office space, furniture, equipment leases, customers, employees already in place! Make sure you and the seller's culture are compatible.

- <u>Business "success" at expense of family, health, faith is really failure.</u> Working 50+ hours a week means something is burning. Fact is, if you are not balanced with things other than work, you will not last anyway. Successful means being successful in more things in life than business! Business is a means to an end, not the end itself!

With failure rates so high it is important to garner what you can. This being said, no list of do's and don'ts ever kept an entrepreneur from forging ahead. Forging ahead is what he does best. If an OE is an animal he is an Alaskan sled dog! On you huskies, on! (huskies being employees here). It may be that the determined OE is going to do what he is going to do, however unprepared. This pride/stubbornness is an element in the 70% failure rate in small business. Don't be so reckless and arrogant, that you run into your own sword or over the cliff.

In 2004 Dun and Bradstreet reported that 88% of all business failures are due to management mistakes. Here is what D&B cited as the main mistakes: going into business for the wrong reasons, underestimate of time needed, pride, lack of market awareness, family pressure on time and funds, and lack of financial awareness. So it should be clear from all the data that venturing into small business ownership is not without significant risk.

But today's job climate is also risky. Ever more so. Lifetime employment, pensions, full medical, and all that are gone. Layoffs out of nowhere are common at large companies. Large companies themselves just disappear. It may be small business is the more stable environment or not much riskier than alternatives have come to be.

My Story

My decision to be an OE occurred at 31. I was in sales for IBM six years and three times Salesperson of the Year in Memphis. One year I was 19th in the country of 4000 reps. I really liked it and thought I would be there forever. I began to specialize in copier products but after a time, IBM got out of them. Being a restless sort I thought I could do really well with a known copier product and become a dealer for it.

I sought the Ricoh copier, but it was taken by an upstart dealer. He already had a partner. I convinced them of what a whiz I was and they sold me a portion for $15,000. I was off. I was an owner.

I did well with the product and never dropped in income from IBM days which were really good. There was nobody telling me what to do or raising quota. I loved it. Let's see. Still had my custom made white shirts and expensive suits. I still felt like shinning my shoes. Some 15 employees worked on my requests and called me "sir". What was there not to like here? Never had all that, even at prestigious IBM. I was feeling pretty chesty even though our office did not have curtains but did have some spider webs.

I was sticking with what I knew, letting things evolve and feeding my predominant trait (independence). I absolutely was Tom "Don't Tell Me What to Do" Pease. That was the most important thing for me. At the same time, it is probably a psychological defect on a chart somewhere.

I brought in most of the money. Larry, majority owner, did whatever owners did and Jerry really didn't do anything. We were always out of money. A year into our deal we got a notice that our doors would be padlocked, since we had not paid payroll taxes for a while. I basically did not even know what that was. I went off on them. I told Larry I did not know what I was going to do, but it probably would not be with them. "Buy me out," was his completely unexpected response. He proposed buying his share which would give me majority. I did for $180,000 with $75,000 down borrowed from a bank. Larry left town the next day and I paid off the rest to him over time. We had revenues of about a million dollars.

After a year it was clear Jerry and I were eggs and ice cream. I caught him writing himself a few too many checks and fired him. Then I bought his ownership. Finally it was just me. Count me as one who would recommend not having partners. They seem like a good idea at the start but later become problematical. They do.

I had a strong sales trait and a tiger eye. That was good to get going but it would not make me last. I needed to hire a good office manager, service manager, and sales manager to get the total expertise and then let them hire the people they needed, as we went along. I did that, as well as attend classes and seminars continuously to keep me up to speed. Whatever their cost, they were always worth it.

I have a suggestion for would-be entrepreneurs or others who will want to own a business. **Before you put your bank account and nervous system on the line, take a job as a salesperson on straight commission**. This is the closest you can come to owning a business yet not risking everything. Being on commission duplicates the situation you have after you quit your day job and declare for entrepreneurship. Straight commission work will tell if you thrive on the challenge of the chase and the success of a much worked for sale. It is a sort of apprenticeship and much safer than going all in before ready. There is no income unless you bring it in. There are competitors doing it, who you have to overcome. Your future income is unknown. All that is close enough.

Sales work is always available too. Especially on straight commission. There is a near 100% certainty that a company would hire you on straight commission to sell their product, if you were already versed in it.

You owe yourself, family, and everyone else vested in you a "trial run" before you risk it all. Straight commission sales work will either confirm your decision to go independent or make you think this is not for you. You have nothing to lose and may save your bank account, marriage, sanity, and ego in the process. Take the sales job first. If you are good at that, you stand a better chance of success and can move into ownership with a degree of confidence. If it is not you, then you have saved yourself and loved ones from a future nightmare. Find out if you thrive on the challenge of a big "zero" in your face and then selling deals that turn that into something beautiful. Find out if you stay energized throughout a day of mostly rejections. Find out if you still look forward to tomorrow facing the same obstacles but still have endless enthusiasm.

Too many OEs, as statistics show, go into business ill prepared. So why do it under such conditions? The carnage of credit standing and financial loss are so large, that licensing standards need to be legislated before one can start, buy or operate a business. The title of this chapter is 'Am I Right For This?" You need to answer that question, even if you are already a business owner.

I have another suggestion to help you before you pass the point of no return. Find three OE's that have been doing it for over seven years. Pitch your situation to them and let their experience answer back with an opinion on your prospects for success.

Answering the "Am I right for this" question is the most critical question to reduce that 70% business failure rate. Accordingly, I have an acid test quiz that gives good clues about the answer to this vital question.

Quiz   1-10

1. I have a high level of passion about doing it.   _____

2. I have knowledge of the product or service.   _____

3. I have rocket fuel in my gas tank.   _____

4. I have worked in sales & liked it.   _____

5. I have identified a product that 'eats & drinks'.   _____

6. I know what my predominant trait is. _____

7. I look forward to forming a team of "A" players. _____

8. I have discussed all with my family. _____

9. I have a detailed plan of some sort. _____

10. I understand positive cash flow. _____

Scoring on this test would be on a one to ten scale with a ten answer meaning the highest degree and one lowest. To save you time, the only correct answer to each question is **ten!** This is the level of commitment and energy necessary to be successful.

Design Elements

Match your business to your personality.   *Stick with what you know.*
Take a sales job first.   *Pass this quiz.*
Did you answer the question?   *Ask three OE's.*

The Owner Must Know
"An investment in education pays the best dividend."

-- Ben Franklin

"You have to know when to hold 'em…know when to fold 'em"…goes the Kenny Rogers song about playing poker. Could be our theme song here. We know that the initial creative bang of entrepreneurial ideas and enthusiasm get many businesses airborne. Then the situation can run out of talent, not always, but we know it happens 70% of the time in small business ownership. Clearly, someone does not know something when they need to know it.

IBM's company motto is *Think*. Their internal company publication is *Think Magazine*. Obviously, they want their people to know stuff. It seems to be working for them.

How about these famous people who knew something when they needed to: John Sullenberg, successfully piloted into the Hudson without a single fatality; George Washington, knowing to push the battle and win America its freedom; George Bush, knowing who and where to attack to avenge 9/11; Steven Jobs, inventing the personal computer/Ipod and know what to do with it.

It has been said that a wise man knows what he does not know. There are none of us, who know it all. We are strong in several areas and weak in others. So have the common sense to bone up in the areas where you do not have a grasp. Drop your pride, ask others, read up, take time to make the decision, dig out historical data, find benchmarks for your industry, and check your 'gut'. The gut is good, because it is your own knowledge, experience and bank of wisdom from previous decisions. But avoid making decisions on how you or somebody else 'feels' or what you heard somebody once 'say'. This happens. Do not make important decisions out of ignorance or based upon feelings. That is GOOB. The owner must know.

There Are Expectations

The position of OE calls for as much professional knowledge as a pilot, doctor or a general because all share a "command" position. These positions, and the decisions made from them, have a large effect on lives and well being. Let's take a look at how large and why it quickly becomes crucial that you know what you need to know.

Picture a gym with you at center court. You are the size of the company day one. Soon you hire employees to be on the court with you. The stands begin to fill with their family members who have an interest in how this team will play. Then you get customers, eventually maybe hundreds, and they take seats in the stands as well.

Next, vendors want seats. Then you need a loan so a banker and his staff want tickets. You need to pay taxes so all city, state and federal agencies arrive soon. Insurance people. Competitors will be in the mix. They will have designs to play against you.

Before long what was just you has the ripple effect of hundreds (thousands?) of people with expectations from you! A Coliseum of Chaos! Certainly you would want to do your very best not to let them down! They may heckle you!

To up the intensity more these individuals have *expectations* of you! "Sell more of my product or else!" says a vendor. "Increase your liquidity if you want a loan!" states your banker. "Where is my promotion?" asks an employee. "Where is my payment?" inquires a supplier. "How come you guys take so long?" a customer wants to know. And so it goes. You did want to be a business owner, though, remember.

Financial

Since it is a business you own, it is reasonable to assume you possess the financial knowledge to run a business and understand the state of its health. Do you?

Do you get financial statements monthly and review them noting changes in any line item and why they are occurring? Your financial statements, both the balance sheet and income statement, are the 'blood work' of a business. These numbers are your company's vital signs. They tell you what is really going on. The most valuable thing they tell you is which way something is trending. Is it increasing or decreasing? The sooner the OE knows something is heading in an unhealthy direction the sooner he can do something about it. This is pretty basic, but there are still plenty of owners who do not get a monthly statement. This is nuts. Know your numbers!

The OE dashboard should have two big dials that read YTD profit/loss position and the company's working capital position, also called the current ratio. Figure it by dividing current assets by current liabilities. The goal is 1.75 to 1.0. If it is less than 1.0, it is indicating not enough cash to pay bills timely. Smaller dials show:

- Checkbook balance. Never take your eye off this one.

- Average collection period. This shows how many days, on average, it takes to collect the money due on an invoice. Take total AR and divide by the annual credit sales and divide by 365. This number needs to be under 45 days and preferably 30 days. If you are cash poor and this number is high, it tells you that you are doing a poor job collecting.

- Inventory turns. This tells how long inventory sits before it is sold. Take cost of goods sold and divide by average inventory. The faster you turn inventory the better your cash flow. If the turnover number is low, say three or four, then you know you have stale paid for inventory which is not selling and is eating cash.

- Debt to equity ratio. This tells you how much of the company you own and how much your creditors, such as banks, "own."

- Return on assets. Figure by dividing net income by total assets. Tells you what the return is from your company from the money you put into it.

- Return on investment. Tells you the degree of profitability. Take net income and divide by book value of assets.

- Total capital. Also known as net worth or book value. This is the difference between total assets and total liabilities. Of course, you want the assets to be more than the liabilities.

- Your pay. You should gross about 12% to 15% of company gross profit.

The key thing in working with ratios or any numerical data is what is their trend? Is this number increasing or decreasing? The trend is more important than the number itself. Trends are early warning indicators of something either heading in the wrong direction or improving. This is key information OE's want. "Am

I closer to Kansas than I was or I am still wandering, Dorothy?" It gives time and data for you to make whatever corrective actions before it is too late. This is mandatory stuff to know to avoid business failure.

Another number, but not a ratio, for OE tracking is AR aging, especially anything over 90 days (accounts deceivable?). An invoice in this column is suspect for collectability. Anything here might have to be written off and hit your P&L statement hard.

Same for stale inventory. You need to know if it is good or not. Inventory paid for and sitting means its value has declined and your P&L with it. To keep from getting stale inventory keep inventories low and order "just in time." In other words, try not to have inventory in inventory!

You must employ a good full charge bookkeeper (one who can compile financials), that gives you accurate numbers and is driven to compile accurate numbers, good or bad. The fate of your business could well hang in the accuracy and timeliness of the information you receive or don't receive. Like a pilot, you need to know the weather ahead, good or bad, and in time, to fly accordingly. It is not necessary for you to know how to compile the numbers, but how to interpret them. If you are uncomfortable a CPA can instruct you or take an accounting course. Again, it makes no sense to be the OE and not know what your gauges are saying, or worse, not to get accurate readings on a monthly basis. Happy ignorance of any of these vital statistics will not cut it either. Sooner or later your lack of information will find you lacking a business. Again, you get a P&L and balance sheet every month and examine them for increases, decreases and trends. This is how you keep your hand on the pulse of the patient.

A good exercise to increase your accounting knowledge is to follow a dollar of revenue through your financial statements. A sale is billed out and lands it on AR, which makes it part of current assets, but has also decreased inventory, and this shows up in cost of goods sold......Do the same exercise for borrowed money and for something that is depreciated. Do this until you understand the impact on both your income statement and balance sheet of any monetary transaction. Once you fully understand this you will think more like a business person which can only help.

Financial knowledge is surely one of the key acumens a business owner should have. Yet, there are those who don't have what they need or figure maybe their bookkeeper is looking after it. Big mistake. It is yours to have and to hold or else you are GOOB.

Legal Matters

Sooner or later you will have to know something about legal trouble. Legal stuff is expensive stuff. Repeat. Legal stuff is expensive stuff. I am no lawyer but I can tell you a few things from the OE view.

If you are being sued, you can relax a little. If the amount is in small claims court, under $15,000, you show up on your trial date and sit until your name is called. You can sit all day and not have it come up until the next day. If your lawyer is sitting with you, well.... Here is an important thing to keep in mind when dealing with your

> *The successful man is the one who finds out what is the matter with his business before his competitors do. .....Roy L. Smith*

lawyer: he works for you and not the other way around. Be clear about what you need and keep him heading in that direction. Do contest charges if you feel they are not justified. Lawyers at larger firms farm out some of their work to other lawyers and the billing can involve others you never meet.

If the amount of the case puts you in the next higher division, it is usually years before the case is settled. This does not mean your lawyer is drawing unemployment during this time. Billing will be around $275 an hour. Cases at these levels are frequently "continued" for the slightest reason. If you are being sued, continuing is good strategy. If you are doing the suing, it will be a long time before you see any money.

Another shocking thing is that the courts have no enforcement mechanism. If you lose and are supposed to pay up, there is no one that makes you do this. There are plenty of judgments against defendants that go unpaid. To force payment is another court session where the judge orders a sheriff to seize property or whatever. Property, that has a lien on it, even if it is seized, cannot be sold without first paying off the lien holder. You may win, but not win anything.

If the parties are in different states it makes matters even more complicated. To sue across state lines means the plaintiff has to come to where the defendant is. This is time consuming and expensive. Also, there could be a continuance, even after traveling all that way. Thus, if someone in another state is threatening to sue, a suit is not likely unless the amount is near $50,000.

If you lose a case you can always appeal. This is your right. You have to post a bond for the damages awarded to the other guy. An appeal is like another continuance. An appeal does not mean you are contesting the whole trial. An appeal is about questioning only a few legal points that took place within the trial, not the whole trial itself. Thus appeals are heard quicker than a trial. You don't have to be there either but your lawyer does. If you know you are guilty you might appeal anyway since this may buy you more time. Then settle the case just before it is heard.

Change Is Coming! Businessaurus Rex!

One of the biggest things a business owner should know is that **things are going to change!** Ipods killed music stores. Cell phones birthed texting. Email killed the USPS. The internet changed everything. Foreign cars killed GM. Computers killed word processors. All the products I sold at IBM—typewriters, dictation equipment, word processors, copiers, and PC's are no longer. Four dollar gas killed truck sales. Digital printing killed printing presses. Terrorism plunged the economy. Newspapers are on the way out. The Iraq war is in the back pages. 401Ks became 104Ks. Enron, Pan Am, TWA, GM, Chrysler, Circuit City, Trump Casinos, Lehman Bros. and endless banks are all bankrupt!

I have no way of knowing what may level your business or mine but it is highly prudent to keep the **CHANGE MONSTER** in mind. He is lurking, always striking somewhere. He is the only two words in this book typed this big. He is to be feared. It is not a matter of if he will appear, only of when. And how angry will he (she?) be? It can get you in the red quicker than any of the other monsters that stalk you.

Change in the marketplace is constant and indiscriminate. The point is you need to be looking for it and find a way to ride it. At least find a way to avoid it knocking you over.

It is fatal and bad design to think things are always going to be as now. Whenever I landed a big deal I would begin thoughts on how we would do once we lost it. Some owners land a few things, start flying high, act like they have received a lifetime contract. They make outlays bigger than they should, and then act amazed when they have the predictable downturn.

I have no crystal ball but here are basics to keeping a business stable or at least decreasing the odds for failure:

➤ Have a strong, bonded work force willing to endure hard times with you.

➤ Be thrifty. Buy used stuff. Do not spend money on anything to create a better image or feed egos. Every senseless dollar out takes one more brick out of your wall. Make sure every dollar helps build something stronger in your business.

➤ Have your customers under some sort of contract, the longer the better. Contracts give you long lead times to better adapt.

➤ Continually work to have good credit lines and have them increased. Then you have them when you need them.

➤ Build bail out factors into your business that can jettison expenses in a hurry. Rent some equipment instead of buying. Keep contracts, such as a building lease, as short as you can.

➤ Constantly look for new markets, products, or services to offer that keep you from having all eggs in one basket. Manage for cash flow. Build up cash. The more you have, the more time you have to ride out hard times.

➤ Have your CPA help you strategize to keep taxes very low. Not just federal income tax but all the state and local ones too. A dollar to the tax man never helped your business so get with a pro to limit this damage but be sure to pay what you owe.

➤ Stay abreast of changes in technology or otherwise. If anything looks threatening the sooner you act the better your chances. Use the advances to make your business more responsive and to reduce employees. Keep training going for all employees.

➤ Increase your company's reliance on service revenue and decrease reliance on hardware sales. Service revenues are more stable. Spending on hard goods is the first thing to go in a downturn because people will use things longer. They will spend more on repair.

➤ Keep your ego out of business decisions. Be guided by good business principles. Period. Ego means loss. A Christian writer said ego stands for Easing God Out.

Businessarus Rex

The Change Monster

It needs to be said as well that things can change *for the better!* You get a great employee you needed. Your product gets more in demand. A competitor closes up. You win a big deal and so on. I think it is best to look at those as bonuses though. It seems, at least in my experience, as well as in the statistics, that the Change Monster comes more frequently as Frankenstein than the Tooth Fairy. But there are more sides than one in there and change can be good. It is like buying insurance. You know things are pretty good most of the time but design against things that can wipe you out.

I recently took in the Broadway play *Fiddler On A Roof.* The fiddler is shown playing beautiful music from a rooftop but is supposed to be subject to the possibility of falling at any time. Why he does not just come down and play from the front porch where it is safe is not explained but hey, this is a very popular Broadway play and you do not question such things. Anyway, the point of the play is that there is beautiful music in everyone's life but it can stop playing at any time. We are all subject to 'falling from the rooftop' at any time. This is a good analogy for business owners. We are all fiddlers on the roof.

Know Where to Spend Your Time

Since the OE is the key asset of the company it is vital that he be deployed to maximize it. It is essential that the OE know where to spend time and where not to. Time management courses teach an ABC thing to decide who does what. The "C" tasks are small taking minutes or hours to accomplish. They may be checking email or getting a haircut. They feel good since they get done. Anybody can do them. The "B" tasks take days or hours to do and not everyone can do them. They require a certain skill, such as how to set up company email accounts or balance inventory. "A" tasks are the mountain movers. They are the OE/president zone of tasks. They require somebody's "A" game-- hopefully you have one by now. They may be the need to find a new location, settle a lawsuit, attain a bank loan, pull the company out of the red, hire a new key manager, increase profits, and decide on a new product line. These projects take weeks and months to settle. "A" tasks are the ones that end up making or breaking a company.

Once these type projects are settled though, they leap the company ahead like solving B and C tasks never will. If your company has one million in revenue then as OE, you have a one million dollar responsibility. If your revenues are two million, then you have a two million dollar responsibility and so on. Does it make sense that you would spend valuable time then on smaller tasks? You never see the brain surgeon admitting patients, the coach putting himself in the game, or the president of the company working the switchboard.

Things like this do happen in small business ownership to its detriment. Sometimes the OE takes the sales floor to save hiring another salesperson or works some in the shop to avoid hiring another technician. This is a great mistake and a design for going out of business. It is either that or you are saying all "A" tasks are accomplished and in hand. Doubtful. If you cannot generate more value than a floor salesperson for your business then you do not belong owning it. Why are you not at work on your "A" tasks? **You delegate all things keeping you from "A" tasks. Then you get to work full time moving your mountains.** I think about Fred Smith, legendary founder of FedEx here in Memphis. He has the same 24 hours in a day I do and he has a global enterprise. I have a Memphis enterprise. Talk about working your "A" tasks. I bet he has never delivered a single package either.

You may remember the movie *Top Gun*. The pilot is Tom Cruise. He and his navigator find themselves in the middle of a horrendous 'dogfight' as they are heavily outnumbered. The navigator, who does not fly in any way, says to Cruise "O.K. time for some of that pilot stuff." Indeed. That is what you, the pilot, is expected to know in times of trouble. Do you?

The bottom line is that the more time an owner spends on "A" work then the more successful the company is going to be. It would not be a bad idea for all OE's to have signs on their desk, or sun visor or bathroom mirror, that say "It's all about the 'A's!"

Parkinson's Law

Parkinson's law states that work spreads itself out to the time available to complete it. This is a principle to remember when trying to determine the head count your business needs to do the job. People are expensive. Payroll is your greatest expense so even one or two extra employees you do not need is costing plenty.

To illustrate, say an employee is working 120% and it is clear there needs to be another hire. If you hire another you have the same 120% workload but two people doing it instead of one. Each one is theoretically at 60%. Months later, if you ask each one about the workload, you will get "covered up boss" as the answer. Hopefully, it is because both employees now have more to do. But you must know if that is really so. The same is true for all your manpower requirements—you must know. In the above case, a better solution is to hire a part time worker to cover the overflow.

The Peter Principle

This one says that every employee will rise to, or be promoted to, their level of incompetence. It means that the last job someone is promoted to is that employee's level of incompetence. It can stay that way. It should be noted that this principle applies to business owners themselves.

This can be improved by giving coachable employees more training and hopefully avoid the Peter Principle. What if it does? Then you have to do what you have to do—lateral move, demotion or out. I have found myself saying, and too many times, that you never really know how someone will do until they get in the job and start doing it. A good thing to do when promoting into a key spot is to say there is probation for three to six months before the appointment becomes permanent. This way everyone understands what is at stake from the beginning and you can limit damage if up against the Peter Principle.

Pareto's Principle

No, all business laws do not start with 'P' but yes, here is another. Pareto's Principle states that the majority of the consequences are brought on by a minority factor. For instance, 80% of the damage was caused by 20% of what went wrong. The Pareto is another name for the 80-20 Rule which you have probably heard. For example, it is known that 80% of most companies profits comes from 20% of its customer base.

The point is to know what these powerful minorities are in your business because they are not so "minor". It is important to make sure you have identified your 20% customer base that brings you 80 % of revenue. This can also be the classic case of "the plane went down because a $5 fastener failed." The space shuttle crashed because a simple piece of foam nicked a wing on takeoff. In a technical area, it can easily happen that all work on something has to stop because you are out of kabonza clips (making that up) for which there is no substitute. Then you be sure you are never out of kabonza clips.

Find Your Benchmarks

For just about every industry there are benchmarks established that lay out the optimum performance standards for that industry. There should be statistics published that tell you how much revenue your business should produce per employee, how much gross profit per dollar of revenue, how much revenue per square foot of floor space, how much service revenue a technician can support, how many units a sales rep should sell, and so on. You may not be able to attain the benchmark but the benchmark numbers are your goal. Normally, if you attain the benchmarks you will be profitable. If there is a trade association for your industry it would have such data. **Know your benchmarks.** They will lead you to profitability and keep you from becoming a benchwarmer. There is a website, bizstats.com, that provides benchmarking information online.

Next time you are making an important decision that involves the well being of people, a significant dollar amount or lengthy contract, ask yourself if you know what you need to know to make the best decision. On what are you basing it? Have you gotten some input from someone with no vested interest? Are you just sort of winging it"? If so, this is GOOB stuff. The owner must know!

There are expectations from you. There are financial statements, ratios, laws, principles, ABC's and change management… and lions and tigers and bears oh no! Oh yes.

Design Elements

There are expectations of you.   *Know your benchmarks.*
Legal is expensive and lengthy.   *Where to spend your time.*
Trend is most important in   *Change Monster Lives!*
financial data.   *The "P" law.*
Work those "A" tasks!

That Owner Frame of Mind

Getting your nose close to
the glass fogs the view

Perhaps you have seen the pictures of the physicist Stephen Hawking who is confined to a wheel chair and paralyzed. Yet, he has come up with some of our greatest theories on the universe from his wheelchair. Go figure. This is a compelling example of the mind's power to rule everything else. The mind of an OE needs to be like this to his business. As much as anything, this book is about getting you to use your mind correctly, to think like a businessperson intent on staying in business.

You may be familiar with the book *As A Man Thinketh*, written in 1902. Here as a passage apropos to our topic:

> *"Mind is the Master Power that molds and makes,*
> *And Man is Mind and evermore he takes*
> *The Tool of Thought, and, shaping what he wills*
> *Brings forth a thousand joys, a thousand ills."*

This is especially true for a business owner. The owner of a business has more levers in front of him than a non-owner that he controls for certain actions. Hire or fire someone today? Get a bank loan? Take on the new product line? Open the new location or not? Reprimand Bill today? Give the pay raises (or cuts)? The outcomes, good or bad, are greater in consequence for a business owner versus a non business owner. Therein lies a lot of satisfaction if you get it right. Therein lies agony if you don't. Much of the outcome is dictated by your thought process or lack of one.

Here is another simple pearl from the same book: **"*Every feeling or action is preceded by a thought.*"** This is also the basis for cognitive behavioral therapy in the counseling world. People are asked to describe their thoughts just prior to seeing a mood or behavior change. These thoughts are key to understanding why someone does what they do. I know this because my wife, Cindy, the counselor, told me so. She has said I do not always have good thought patterns and, that if this book is published, she said she will write the sequel 'Survive Living With An Entrepreneur'. One of her most memorable lines is her take on the classic thing of seeing the glass half empty or half full. She says I do not see the glass.

Same is true for businesspeople. We need to make sure we get a clear view of what our thoughts really are. That we actually see the issues clearly before making decisions. It is important to get other informed thoughts to go with ours, especially from people without a vested interest. Then wait a week before you decide. This process makes for a better decision maker and helps you make fewer mistakes.

The more years under his belt the more cerebral the OE should get. Tasks should be well delegated by now and the OE busy contemplating solutions to 'A' projects or creating new designs to be carried out for the good of the business. The chapters in this book that compile Part One are basically chapters to form good brainwork. This book is all brainwork (possibly open to discussion) written from a nearly 100% compilation occurring in my mind first and then typed out for, hopefully, people's benefit.

For your mind to benefit your business it needs to be continually fed with bits (or bytes?) of information that only you can process to a conclusion that works for your enterprise. I always got some of my best information from walking around yakking with my people. You get different business perspectives from admin people versus tech people versus sales people. You need them all to come to good judgments about what is or is not going on in your company and with your customers. What is more important than those things? You cannot get that kind of input by being isolated. So take it all in, process it in your Pentium brain for days or weeks, and then do something brilliant!

But On Most Days

Processing grand company plans in your Pentium brain is surely the best use of it but most of the time there is everything else but that going through it consuming valuable creative neuron juices. Who can blame it though? This is small business ownership we are talking, not The Einstein Think Tank with Beethoven playing background while people sip wine.

The OE wakes in the morning, assuming he did sleep, wondering how he is going to pull himself out of the red *this year*. "Well, half way through the year and running red. Nobody seems to have money or to be buying anything. I just put in that new computer system. Why? The new salesperson seems like a bust. I am supposed to give him more time and money I don't have. Lost that big deal we were hoping to close this month. An auditor is coming to check workman's comp."

And this is just the first five minutes of thought process for the day.

It is easy to fill yourself with this stuff and it is unavoidable. It is part of the responsibility. You have a lot of company, not that

that solves your issues. While too much worry is not a good thing a lack of pressing objectives isn't either. Most OE's live off these challenges and it helps keep their brain in a certain state of fitness. I know I get bored easy and problems give me opportunities to be creative.

I have found that one of the most uplifting things, no matter what is going on, is to get with my employees at a company pot luck luncheon and just take in the conversations and interplay. For the most part, none of it has to do with business and it is just people being people, laughing, cutting up. I tend to marvel, still, that I have come to be their center of the universe for employment matters and family breadwinning. The day before I may have been thinking I could stand to lay off a few but this is mainly because I just want relief from my pressures **right now** and am not using any patience. The lunch gathering has a way of fueling my thought process. I then just feel more confident about the whole thing and go about my business in a more positive manner.

So this is where I am at lunchtime, four hours later.

The lunches are great and I try to hop around and eat with various employees. "How did it go at Jones Bros.?" I ask a sales rep. "Oh, like most of my week not that productive. Those people just do not get how bad they need our machine." Great. What does Norman Vincent Peale say to think now, I wonder. "But I am going to close a good size deal next week at Stevens." All right then. This is better I say to myself. Ride the roller coaster. This is what I do.

Moving along I land next to my service manager. "Hey Theo, what is the latest?" I ask. "Well, I think Johnny is getting a divorce. He is down and unhappy and I have been getting complaints. He said he was having problems at home. This is why he is not here." Not too much heavier things than marital problems so one of my guys is loaded down worse than me. I ask to see him. I will see what I can do.

Helping an employee, is a big way to get your mind in a good place. As an employer, as I mention elsewhere, you are in a position to assist your people in little ways and sometimes big ones. There is probably no shortage of need so you always have good you can do for someone else if you are sagging. It works for you both. A win-win.

Well, lunch is over so I chat with my controller. She mentions some bad AR we need to write off, that F&E taxes are due next month and are up to $7000. Oh boy, why doesn't somebody just waterboard me today? Further into the visit the office manager sticks her head in the door and announces that we forgot to bill Acme company last month somehow. She is embarrassed and feels bad. "Hey, that's great" I respond. There was about $10,000 gross profit in that. Some great news there." Well, this cancels out the F&E taxes anyway.

Occasionally you get something odd and funny —some comic relief. We had our truck driver deliver a machine and he was to pick up a check for it for $18,000 which he did. On the way back he rolled down his window for a moment and the check flew out the window and down the interstate.

Dealing With Darkness

This is a typical up and down day repeated endless times throughout the year—so much so that small business ownership could be classified as a bipolar disorder. The point is to not get too close to the details, to protect your valuable 'A' brain. Find techniques that work for you but do find some. It is not a luxury but a necessity. Train your young people to think "I am busy protecting my boss's 'A' brain! Yes, my boss, the 'A' brain dude!" I again thank my assistant, Debe, who excels in dealing with detail.

The OE mind will have its share of dark days and weeks. I have had more than I can count. Stuff can just get to be too much at times, heavily concentrated in the negative (pick from anything in the Managing Trouble chapter). Of course nothing attracts more negativity than negativity. If you have three really bad things going on, you can count on your mind serving up ten more on its ticker tape! This Law of Negativity does not seem to work with positive thoughts, for some reason. I think it takes about five positive thoughts to cancel out one negative.

All these down periods are brain power outages. They make you as dysfunctional as a home in a thunderstorm. I have learned things from experiencing these shades of gray. The first is it takes others to get you out of them. Let them in. Let them suggest. Tell them how you feel. Be humble. Don't be prideful. Right there is half the battle. Employees should be a source of support for you like you are for them. Try to lead them onto the comeback trail with a slogan or campaign. If you can get your workforce to give you another ten percent effort this can be a significant source of energy to bring the needed improvement. "Can You Give Me Another Ten?" may be your slogan to kick things off. The other half of the battle is to know it will pass.

Hopefully you have a stress management program to go to during pressing times. A hobby or exercise are both great if not a necessity. Restore your juices by laying down your load for a time. If you hold a baby long enough you will stress your arms to the point the pain and fatigue require you to lay the baby down to prevent worse things from happening. Once you have done that for a time, you will be able to pick it back up again! The same is true for you and business stress.

The OE frame of mind has to be working six to twelve months ahead. What does it look like if we lose a large account? What does it look like after we pay off that loan? What does it look like if customers ease up on buying service contracts? What does it look like if our salespeople do not do better? What does it look like if someone else takes on our product line? What does it look like if we open in another city? Yes, in addition to your other duties, you are responsible for telling the future.

It is hard to see the big picture if your nose is against the glass. This fogs it up and you do not have a clear view anymore. It really is a constant struggle to deal with today and still have a clear enough brain to see some tomorrow. You have to do both but you do multi-task don't you?

The OE's brain cells have to be heavily invested in passion for his business, to be able to burn rocket fuel, or else there will be problems. Again, I address the creative model of entrepreneurship, not the managerial or self employed models. You can go a long, long time on your passion and then you most likely have run low on the fuel and need another one. Or, find a new way to get new passion out of your old business.

One way to do this is to be driven by teaching your subordinates the ropes and cheering for them like you did at your kid's ball games. Their youth and vigor is hopefully the passion the business needs to spur it along without you serving as the propellant.

I sound a little more on the gloomy side with this chapter. There is a lot of time when things are going well. When they are, sit back and say to yourself 'It is good to be King!' (Queen). It sure is. It is good to be valued by many people such as your customers, your insurance agent, banker, CPA, lawyer, employees, AT&T, American Express etc. etc. All these people are on your side and appreciate you for your contribution to their well being. Some may even curry your favor. It feels good to do well and know you are coming through for a lot of people and not just yourself.

Nobody fires a King or Queen so that is a perk. You can come and go as you please. Your subjects will greet you with respect. As it should be. Nobody can tell you what to do or else you can have them beheaded. You can have assistants take care of all the 'little things' that annoy you that regular people must take care of themselves. So it is Good to Be King despite the fact forces may plot to overthrow you or that there is that fire breathing dragon outside the castle walls waiting to spew flames on you.

In summary we can say that the business owner's mind is a highly driven, creative thing that does many good works and enjoys distinct periods of happiness and satisfactions. It makes jobs, careers, innovations, and money. At the same time, it suffers unique mental traumas and black holes normal humans do not! It needs to be able to tell the future. It must also be able to look at a checkbook, without passing out, that may have no money in it. This mind needs to see that it is its own worst enemy and a part of the competition. It must keep its ego in check or else be cited for business **DWI—deciding while intoxicated**. It must do all this living with the knowledge there is a 70% chance the business will not even exist seven years from now. This is why entrepreneurs are admired.

Other than that…phew! Still, at any given time, there are millions of OE's out there. It is safe to say too, that at any time there are a lot of them in some form of pain or anxiety. This is kept at bay by passion, sense of mission and rocket fuel. Special creatures for sure.

It is time for recognition to acknowledge and protect the contributions OE's make while dealing with such uncertainty. Let's start with a new psychiatric disorder, business DWI, and have medical schools train specialists to help save ourselves from ourselves. Then we need the Bank of Po' Cash Flow to loan small businesses money when it looks like you shouldn't. Since we always have trouble and are constantly troubled, we need our own church patron. Our Lady of Turmoil might be good. For the spouses and close supporters there should be a self help group. I suggest TA for the Traumatized Anonymous. Finally, there needs to be a new cabinet level position created—Secretary of the 70%--to work on cutting that failure number down!

I don't know where you are in your career but I want to see you well past the seven year point and happily designing for retirement with a frame of mind that awards you due satisfaction. Mine is here and working fairly well for the past five years. I asked my VP what she would write on my tombstone after these 29 years of small business combat, the up and down and all around. She said: 'He Broke Even'.

I'll take it. It has given me a great income, a privileged life, relationships with wonderful people, and continues to do so even though it still gets into its share of trouble. But it serves me more now and I serve it less. As it should be. As it should be.

How Am I Leading?

"Leadership is both something you do and something you are."

Fred Smith, FedEx

Since you cannot do everything you hire employees. Their success depends a lot upon your leadership. Leading means being out front. Employees expect to find you there with great inspiration, incentives, motivation, and answers to their training needs. They expect you to communicate well and frequently.

In this chapter I will tell you what I think is the big secret in establishing and continuing to have a successful small business.

To be an inspirational leader you stand for things and are known for them. Quick. Write down the most important business principles you have. If you asked your employees would they be able to echo these? These principles need to be repeated frequently and fervently—like battle cries.

With all the technology you can pick your medium from email, voice mail, snail mail, text messaging, company luncheon, company newsletter or website. Pick what is comfortable and use the heck out of it. Communicating is leading. "I am very pleased to see that our standard of 35% gross margin is being met by all the salespeople." "I am saddened to know Mary has lost her Father and I *expect* us all at the funeral." "My stated response time to customers of four hours or less has not been quite that and I want it improved." These might be some mantras to repeat.

What makes a good leader? This is not easy to define. Somerset Maughan, the author, said: "There are three things that define a good leader. I just don't know what they are."

Communicating is Leading

To be a leader you must be a communicator. I repeat, communicating is leading. The CEO should be a lighthouse beam constantly putting out comm that illuminates. The best advice ever given on how to communicate is from **Confucius: "Tell me and I will forget. Show me and I will remember. Involve me and I will understand."**

Poor communication is toxic to profits. To satisfied customers. To tenured employees. To equanimity. To having fun. Get the picture? If you are not a communicator best to stay with a small number of employees and customers because this will ensure it. Obama led the nation on election day primarily because he could really talk. Try taking a Dale Carnegie course if you are unsteady. On the other hand, my wife Cindy, a counselor, reminds me that half of good communicating is listening. She says she is not always impressed with the listening skills of men. Chauvinist!

To lead you need to communicate well and often. State what you stand for over and over, be clear, be out front, visible, vocal, inject the positive, be inspirational and be empathetic to the individual. Over and over. **Be A broken record? Yes**. Advertising research shows it takes continual repetition for the mind to absorb a message. Worse, once messages are received they are forgotten over time. If you are, instead, unclear, reclusive, unavailable, change your mind a lot, moody, cannot listen nor work with personal needs, you will not be a good leader, nor a communicator and be GOOB.

Good leadership puts the fuel in employees' tanks *especially when you are not there.* They hear your guiding principles in their heads as they work with customers and co- workers. If you have done a good job with the comm, then you are always there even when you are not there. It means you are in on each sale even though you are not. If your leadership is good, employee results should be similar. If not, your employees will wander like a tribe without Moses.

If you have 30 employees you have 30 personal lives coming in the door: parenting, marital, health, financial and romantic concerns. The point is personal problems do not stay home. They come to work. This is just human nature. On top of this you have other tensions such as admin types not understanding sales types and tech types not liking anything other than tech. It seems humans tend to talk towards the negative. All this consumes valuable company business oxygen.

Thus a priority leadership objective is to *continually* inject positive juoo juoo into the atmosphere. It must be powerful and is so highly needed because, for some reason, one negative thought is more powerful than five positive ones. Employees carry many negative thoughts toxic to company morale and profitability. You can never have too many positive elements going to counter negative ones going on with employees and maybe you too. What can get this done? Good managers who do a good job of leading is the best answer. I also like company newsletters, bowling nights, softball teams, monthly pot luck luncheons where employees are praised, company picnics, and annual company recognition banquets where employees are really praised. We have had company go kart nights. Send a hand written Christmas card each year. All positive vibes from events are money in the piggy bank of the owner who will always need them to counter some crises. You don't do it to "get" something. I actually do it to give something.

The big point here is that to get the most out of your workforce you need to be close to them and they to you. The business owner loses needed power if he and the workforce are not a solid, united band of brothers and sisters ready to take on come what may.

As Chief Morale Officer you should have fun. Issue company jackets, hats or golf shirts with your company logo. Same for pens and portfolios. Here's one. At your monthly luncheon play Company Trivia. Ask a lot of trivia questions about your company, its products and people. Each correct answer pays $10. Money carries over to next employee if answer is wrong. The questions can assist in keeping employees current on products. My favorite was "spell facsimile" since we sold fax machines.

The Big Secret

IBM has a key tenant called "Respect for the Individual." All employees are told they can count on it. It means any employees' needs will be understood and taken into consideration. In a large company, though, even if the understanding is there it cannot "bend" the rules of the company for anyone that needs it. Large companies have lengthy employee handbooks which spell out all the do's and dont's.

This tenant, meaning respect the individual, I have found to be magic in small business leadership by taking it a step further. In essence, in small business, a leader/manager should **treat everyone** *differently!* For instance, working mothers have high stress over a child in day care. I made it policy they could leave without notice if their child was ill at day care and stay home with them and not be docked. I was taken aback by the amount of respect and admiration I got from that. Not fair to non-mothers? Well, believe me, everyone has something that needs wiggle room. Find it. Give it. In that sense, everyone is treated equally after all.

Treating everyone differently, my friends, is the great secret to successfully running a small business. It has been for me anyway. Treating everyone differently is something only a small business can do. It leads to greener bank accounts for all as well as greener pastures. It is your great advantage! Use it! It is really a form of problem solving. Use your company, and its extra muscle, as one big problem solving mechanism for its workers. All employees, being individuals, vary in what holds them back, frustrates them, pleases them, scares them, bores them and so on. When you know your employees well, you know what these things are. Then you can start working with that and create grateful and then super motivated staff.

In essence, the OE is marketing himself and his company to the employees first. Most marketing today tries like crazy to get a breakdown of its customers so that it can better respond to them. For example, if you buy groceries at Kroger you have Kroger card that gives you a discount for the privilege of Kroger looking at every purchase you made and weighing it against your personal data. Same principle here.

It seems the phrase 'treat everyone fairly' or 'treat everyone equally' is in our culture from somewhere. It is fine as it goes but falls short of doing a better job by knowing more about them. Just ask Kroger or all these marketing research companies. We know that you treat a male and a female differently. One treats a teenager differently than a grandmother. It just makes sense to try and find the little things for each individual that, yes, are not done for someone else, but that mean a great deal to an employee. This gives you a more loyal employee and a more satisfied one. The fun is that the one who may gripe has his turn come up soon enough and that ends all dissent.

If I am working with an employee who has a 30 minute commute each way I try to adjust him a bit. It has great meaning. It will have no meaning to the employee who lives a mile away but maybe he has some issue about needing to pick his kid up when baseball practice is over. You accommodate both. Big deal. Everybody is happy.

To be successful in sales means you have to identify business problems and solve the *particular* needs of the customer with what you do or sell. This is the same concept behind treating everyone differently. It will get you a better result than treating everyone the same. Treating everyone the same just seeks the middle as its goal. Wouldn't it be better for your business if you got a strong pulse out of all your employees? I think the concept of 'treat everyone equally' came about from lazy business owners.

Back to those working mothers. Their children are always on their minds and nothing is more dear. If you can work schedules so they can pick the kids up from school you have a friend for life. I offer to let them off an hour early, without pay, but usually they come back and say they will work through lunch if that would be OK. Sure.

My service department has a bunch going at it with endless sports talk. We have had several softball enthusiasts who have played on church teams. I asked one if he would like to head up a company team, coach it, get us in a league, get us uniforms. You would have thought he was just drafted by the N.Y. Yankees.

I had a technician with five kids whose wife got ill and couldn't work anymore. Of course their money was stretched and she eventually got disability income. In the process, their central air went out. Memphis in the summer may as well be Africa. My assistant told me about this and that the family was miserable with all those kids in a hot house. I went to him and said that if he would take a few machines home to work on at his convenience (we rebuild machines) I would get him new central air.

Young families with children, and we have had our share, are tight for money and nice vacations are not in the cards. I pictured a company cabin on a lake that employees could use at no charge for a decent family vacation. I managed to get a mortgage for one in a nice area. Employees could book it for a week and pay nothing. It was a big hit and did a lot for the families. It was in the company name and basically an investment. Ten years later, and after many, many good days there, the kids had grown up and we sold it with a nice profit, some of which was distributed at the Annual Awards Banquet.

Our business is in the South—The Bible Belt. I am a Catholic and have had other committed Christians work at my company. One was the zealous type and near street preacher. I thought it a good thing, for those that wanted to, if we started the day with ten minutes of Bible verse followed by a bit of discussion. I knew I would participate but it would not be good for the owner to be driving a religious event. I asked Earl the

> *"Treating everyone differently is a great secret to successfully running a small business."*

Zealot, if he would help me form this group and be its "leader." You know his next words if you live in the south: "Praise God! Yes I will." It did well for five years. Then for some reason we didn't do it anymore. But Earl was in his glory.

We have schools for our technicians and admin people that can last a week. When in a nice city I would ask if they would like the spouse or relative to go along at no extra cost. They can make a bit of a vacation of it.

I could go on but you have the idea. None of these are expensive. I am sure I make money on them from the most dedicated and loyal employees an owner could want. Certainly the employees returned the same treatment to me and the company. Most willingly put in extra hours and go the extra mile for the customer. What better design ingredient could top that one for staying in business year after year?

Since, as I said, I believe this to be a major key in my success, and in yours, here are more ideas you can use:

While sorting through particular needs **become the Employee Godfather**. Just like in the movies but no horse heads in beds. You make "deals" employees cannot refuse.

- Those "deals" may be financial such as an employee loan. **Judge these carefully but a compassionate employer can help a beleaguered employee.** I once loaned my receptionist $5000 to pay off her Sears bill. It bore 29% interest and she could not get out from it. I charged 5% and payments came out of her check so repayment wasn't a problem. You might advance an employee money that would be totally paid back from their next check. Your power of the paycheck is assurance of being paid.

- Make it known employees can use company assets like the lift gate truck if they need to move. If you have an old desk, chair, table, workbench, vacuum, cabinet, tool, refrigerator or things like it not being used offer them free to employees, maybe the younger ones with families.

- Let employees barter a company product to help secure a major purchase. For example, if a new air conditioner is needed the employee can pay our company wholesale for an office copier, and then trade the usual profit margin to his air conditioner company (if they can use a copier). That is money off the employee's bill at no cost. A good used machine can work even better.

- Round up employees available once a week and take them all to lunch on the company. Great fun and rapport building. Worth the cost.

- Help an employee with a hospital stay. The insurance deductible--usually a thousand dollars-- is paid by the employees and a company contribution. It is not much per person and saves the patient a big headache.

- Do all you can to remove obstacles that keep them from doing a better job. Buy them a new computer, a faster printer, a better desk chair. It shows you care and well you should.

- Feel out work schedules and propose flex time. Maybe an employee faces unbearable traffic on the way in or home and a one hour later start will be gold. Another loves to pick up their child from school at 4:00. It may be that there are jobs that can be worked just as well from home with a remote computer terminal. Accommodating these employees with different hours endears you beyond all money. Do it. You need it for your piggy bank.

- Have a Movie Day. Once in a while send all your inside people to the movies. Inside people are "deskbound" and do not get the outside freedom of service and sales types so this is what I do to "get them out". It is inexpensive and wildly uplifting. Going to the movies on company time! Who does that? Outside employees come in to answer the phone.

- Have skeleton days. When a holiday weekend approaches or any other slow time of the year a full crew is overkill. I retain a skeleton crew so everyone else can be off with pay. Thanksgiving, Christmas, New Years etc. are good times to do this.

- Make good use of company cars. If you pay mileage think about leasing company cars instead. Employees view this as a huge perk. It is about the same cost to you. It can retain employees too since they usually sell their car and if they wanted to leave you they would have to buy a car to do so. Let them pick the color.

Displaying Leadership

Work hard *for* your employees. In your mind make it as if you work *for* them. The fact is, you need them worse than they need you. Act like it. I am always humbled they choose to cast their lot with me. They can always get another job. I can't. Be The Godfather with company resources and maximize them for the employees' benefit. All this creates a valuable employee bond which is more powerful than money and especially helpful when the company itself gets into distress, which it will. Your Band of Brothers and Sisters will then be there for you and that will make all the difference.

Don't forget appearances send leadership messages. Make them the right ones. As CEO, your attire should be a cut above the others—always clean and pressed. Your car washed. Your workspace clean and uncluttered. These things signal confidence from the top. The message you don't want to subtly send is that you can't manage yourself so how will you do it with others? Go around and greet each employee each morning. Enthusiasm should spill out of you.

A leader must have a vision and make it a part of the employees' vision. What do you see for your employees? What are you willing to commit to their further business education? What products or services do you see for customers? How much area do you want to cover? What are you going to offer to get good hires? What is your message going to be? What will you say in advertisements or on your website? All vision things. Write down your vision(s) and boil them down to three or four good sentences. Communicate this to your troops.

Recognition is an essential element of leadership. I have had annual awards banquet that cost $15,000 including cash awards, the dinner, and most importantly, great plaques. Awards include the sales, technician, and admin persons of the year. We have the employee of the year as voted on by the employees. There is the rookie of the year. There are 10 year and up service awards. The highlight is a slide show of pictures taken all year for this purpose. Speeches are given. At Open Mic anyone can talk. Invite your banker if you have had a particularly good year.

I begin banquets, as I do the company luncheons, with a prayer. I give the first recognition to my wife for her support. All these things constitute my leadership values and how I highlight them in a way others might give thought to as well.

When it comes to leadership effectiveness remember you cannot give what you do not have. If you are not confident about a new product you will not inspire confidence in others. If you have not put good content and practice into a company address it will not come off as a moving experience. Give yourself what you need whether it be more practice, more education, more reading, more listening, more data gathering, more empathy, so that what you "give" is something you have. If you are genuine and possess actual knowledge of what you are talking about you will do well. I am good at teaching copier sales since I did it. So it shows. But if I need to instruct on compiling financial statements I will be two sandwiches short of a picnic since I do not have that ability and it would show. When you are in leadership mode make sure you are bringing it with you as well as "bringing it."

Most followers do not like leaders who are cocky and self-congratulatory. Sincerity and honesty should rule an effective leader. Admit mistakes. Admit your limitations. Admit you don't know if you don't. In short, admit it! People gravitate to these qualities. It makes you more effective. You will not be effective if people are mentally tuning you out. Picture a football huddle. When you are in tune with your people they are pulled in with you, shoulder to shoulder so to speak. But when you are ego driven, superficial, and a know- it- all, then your employees are going to look like a huddle does when it breaks.

A young entrepreneur had just moved into new quarters. Customers and employees were standing around his office. He was proud and went into his office and picked up the phone. He talked quite animatedly, gesturing and talking large deals. A visitor soon tapped on his door. Can I help you? "Yes sir, I am here to hook up your phone."

A popular leadership model is to be more like a coach than a boss. Encourage, motivate, teach, compete, practice a lot, never give up and revel in any victories. Sounds good to me.

Ego is Expensive

If you are an ego juiced person, or if ego is present in your decision making process, stop there! **My experience shows when ego is involved in decision making it is going to *get expensive for someone,*** hopefully not you. I will go so far as to say that any business or business decision based on satisfying an owner's ego will come undone.

I once bought a competitor because he was in serious trouble and asked if we could work something. We did. We signed the usual non-compete agreement to go with the deal and he was to work for my company a year. It was a bitter pill since he lost his company, much less to a competitor, and someone years younger. From day one his ego got the best of him as he subtly tried to undermine us to make himself look better. After eight months, incredibly, he went to work for a competitor while being paid $7000 monthly on his purchase price. He said he was justified in doing so but never said how. He revisited and tried to re-sell old customers he had sold to me. Once that happened I stopped his $7000 and, of course, he took me to court. The judge was incredulous at his behavior and ruled for me in the amount of $425,000.

Another time I had a builder submit a proposal for a construction loan. The builder visited city hall, got regulations, and quoted $30 a square foot. I applied for the construction loan and got approval. A few weeks later the builder announces he made a mistake and it will cost $50 a square foot.

I cannot believe it nor the bank which had to go back to square one. Of course I fire the builder and get another. The original builder wants $35,000 for his trouble and for the architect and engineer. I decline since he has cost me a lot in time aggravation and money. I am thinking he owes me. I offer something for his architect and engineer if they finish the job.

Ego Builder says it is all or nothing or he is suing for a lot more. "See you in court" is my response. After many delays and six years, yes six years, the court awards the builder, architect and engineer zero.

Senior employees can work their way into becoming people with ego issues. They feel their 'rank' warrants them something and that they are to be dealt with. They are looking for some homage to be paid. It gets to be more and more about themselves, about winning, and less about the actual well being of the company. Ego heads start deciding who they are for or against and try to maneuver others into their way of thinking. These people are pure business cancer and do about as much damage eventually. At the heart of it seems to be some lack of self esteem or other mental illness. When you begin to see signs of this in an employee right now is not even soon enough to give a stern warning. It only gets worse if left unchecked. The opposite of ego is humility. These people need doses of it.

When I was doing well selling for IBM I would get a little cocky at times. My mother would be quick to say "Pride goeth before a fall, Tommy." Good business advice. Although she did not know a lick about business she did know what got people in trouble.

Men are very prone to egoism. It is in the male DNA. If male '1' says he sees three bass swimming in the lake male '2' will say he sees at least 10. In business, men will throw around numbers that sound impressive and always bigger than the last number they just heard anyone else speak. There can be endless circles of b.s. among men in companies (some women too) and it does not impress anybody. It is really a form of lying and lying destroys credibility—every businessperson's valuable asset.

Ego problems cost so very, very much. The ego issue causes the failure of some businesses and is a factor in the 70% failure rate. This is truly a serious design flaw. There are many owners out there who are ego maniacs. This is equivalent to building a foundation on sand. They commit business **DWI—Deciding While Intoxicated**. Keep yourself out of that zone—practice some humility when you can is a good way to do this. If you are, in fact, ever at fault—own up soon! But if your opponent is on an ego driven drive, relax, and brace for the crash.

Ego maniacal CEO's, and employees, from Wall Street to Main Street, have destroyed entire businesses, and people's lives with them, due to exercising their egos and committing DWI. Do we doubt for one minute recent Wall Street collapses, have, as their root cause, serial DWI-ing CEOs ensconced in Taj Mahal offices with mega million dollar salaries whether they do the job or not? Are we surprised they are GOOB because of this? Have we yet to hear any say they made mistakes or errors in judgment? No, because they would actually have to be capable of some humility and compassion to do this. How is it taught that to 'up the other guy' or 'appear superior' is success in life? It is absolute failure. Do your best and let it rest.

Let us call it what it is—the gravest vanity of them all –pride. My mother did have it right as mothers usually do. Even my children, when they were young, knew it. They didn't know they knew but by flashing a big 'L' on their forehead for Loser, they signaled the defect. The Bible says pride is the deadliest of the capital sins. I am no Bible scholar but I can vouch for that. Stay humble! It seems so obvious yet people cannot do it.

Good Leader?

How good a job are you doing as a leader? Find out. Once a year compile a questionnaire with 15 questions that measure you on a one to ten scale or an "improving" or "getting worse" checkmark. Have questions meaningful to you such as "How would you rate the level of trust and confidence you have in the President" or "How well do you think you are understood by the President". Of course answers are anonymous. You get a financial statement monthly so it is wise to get a leadership statement annually. You know the management axiom **"You can't manage it if you don't measure it."** Measure up! Measure everything!

At some point you have to decide how and where you are leading yourself. Are you enjoying managing people or not? Are you enjoying the "craft" of your business more than anything else? Are you enjoying the creating of things—new products and new markets—more than anything? You really cannot be all of these effectively. If you have been in business a while it is time to decide which tree you want to climb.

To be entrepreneurial means you prefer the creation route. To be happy you will have to feed yourself plenty of new stuff and delegate the old stuff, especially details. You will need to work more through your managers. You will want to grow and stay excited by things. Your staff will need to be skilled enough to handle day to day so you can be free to be free.

If you prefer the performance of your craft more than anything it is best to stay "hands on" and under 10 employees. You would be termed "self-employed." If you enjoy management then you will prefer being "in charge" and in touch day to day. You will be a good delegator but still need a diet of details and control mechanisms.

These are all fulfilling roles but it needs to be clear which one is you.

Design Elements

Review Confucius's Communication.	*Treat Everyone Differently.*
Become Employee Godfather.	*You work for the Employees.*
Can't Give What You Don't Have.	*Measure It.*
Keep Ego Out of It.	*Provide Recognition.*

Your Biggest Competitor
I have seen the enemy and it is me.

All OEs need to realize that their biggest competitor is not that company across town. It is themselves! Their own company! That's right, you are the competition to be most concerned with. There is more money to be made by winning the battle against yourself than there is by beating a competitor. How so? By bringing sloppy operations up to par and by overcoming all the resistance built into each of us that stifles creative force. **Creativity is a must for all entrepreneurs.** Problems cry out for it and problems need to be just fertilizer for the solutions that are supposed to pour from the OE brain.

The creative element should be a big part of why you want to be an OE in the first place. You want to see where your talents and drive will take you. What you can create with nobody holding you back but yourself. If, in fact, this element is not a part of what led you here then this is a strong sign you are more oriented to being self-employed than anything else. You may want everybody to just leave you alone with your craft. Fine, but this book is aimed at the entrepreneurial model of business ownership.

You Must Create

The better you are as a creator then the tougher it is on your competition to duplicate what your company does. You need to 'out create' the competition. For example, could anyone tell Steve Jobs how to create the Ipod? Could he find that in any book? Can anyone tell Paul McCartney how to sing? Can you tell an artist how to paint? The answer is no. Creating something means you took existing elements and made something unique. Nobody can really tell one how to do this. How, you say, are you supposed to do something that has never been done before? Easier than it sounds. All these artists took things that already existed—computer chips, musical instruments, paint—and made them do something unique. You do the very same when

> *".....making decisions while juiced up on some sort of ego trip is business DWI--deciding while intoxicated."*

you take your existing elements—your employees, products, services—and do something unique. You put your unique twists and execution to them, combined with yourself as chief creator. Then there it is. Or isn't. This is why you get the big bucks. Or at least the big responsibility. Uncreative, 'me too' solutions, do not pay well and lead to slow GOOB anyway.

I grew up in Wisconsin where it always snowed. Shoveling your driveway was as common as taking out the garbage. Dad never did shovel the driveway although he cleared it regularly. Dad attached plywood to the front bumper of the family car (a VW). He would circle the house to get up a head of steam and blast the snow off the driveway. With a few good swoops, he was finished. I did not ever see anyone else's dad do this even though they had cars too and could get some plywood. It was unique. While neighbors were still out scooping snow dad was back inside watching the Green Bay Packer football game.

There it was. Dad solved his problem with swoops while others scooped. He had the creativity to think of this solution. He overcame the 'resistance' of circling his home with the family car while affixing plywood to its front bumper. But heck, once he got past that, he was miles ahead of everyone else. In his creative process he gained competitive advantage against the snow by learning swoops were a lot more powerful than scoops. Hopefully the illustration is clear.

This is close to the way an OE has to think to get miles ahead. You have to put yourself out there and not worry how it looks at the moment. Instead, is it moving me miles ahead? Am I swooping or scooping? For example, maybe you can rent some space in a high traffic area and put up a manned display to the public. It will bring needed exposure for your business. Yet you are squeamish about being so in the public. Maybe you hide, instead, behind some small print ads in a publication. That is scooping instead of swooping. It is resistance to something that might move you miles ahead. Step out there.

It may surprise you that all this is, in fact, rocket science. As was once explained to me in consulting school rocket science is about thrust. Thrust is about propulsion and propulsion is about overcoming gravity. There you are. Once you overcome your "gravity" you can lay claim to knowing some rocket science. Back to earth let's try and find some more areas where your resistance is your own worst competitive force.

Have you increased expertise to qualify for more business in the market place? Maybe you miss new business because you do not have that Microsoft MSCE or Master Plumber or graphic artist. That is your fault. As your business grows why have you not grown your expertise when it means more business? Salespeople are a big source of a company's revenues. Do you have a stable of racehorses or a pasture of donkeys? You can be steadily increasing sales training, recruiting and recognition but you aren't. The extra revenue from a more focused effort will be more than you would win from lowering prices to beat the competition.

Just being profitable and paying bills timely will win you important muscle to increase business and has nothing to do with a competitor. Have you accomplished this yet? If so, banks will loan you what you want so you can expand your business—maybe to another city. Again, moves like this bring much more than beating a local competitor in some deals would. The loan gods will also loan you money to buy your competitor based upon your good history. Think about this one. Think about that "victory" over a competitor and its additional business. But more than that, running a disciplined, stable business, adhering all the while to sound business principles when others are about operating otherwise, is real accomplishment. If you cannot say this then you are still beating yourself.

You are the Designer in Chief. *The job of the OE is to design for the big money.* You are not supposed to sell, you are to develop the structure and personnel to sell. You are not supposed to repair things but to hire the technicians and develop your company's ability to repair other products. When the OE is taking on either of these roles he is selling himself too cheap and hurting his company's ability to compete in the marketplace and not really doing his job. If you have extra time on your hands you need to spend it seeking other areas of Big Money such as finding a company to buy or a new market to enter.

Improving Your Ability to Compete

The average company loses three to five percentage points on total revenue from sloppy and careless operation. Areas where there is a lack of focus or control hurts your bottom line and has nothing to do with competitors. It is you shooting you. Improving internal deficiencies is like lifting weights to get the body in shape but this is your company we are trying to strengthen. Shall we take a closer look?

Inventory. What is the dollar amount of inventory that has not moved in six months? One year? Whatever it is it is the result of poor judgment or misjudging the market. The task is to keep this from happening. Make better judgments. This inventory is devalued by now. It is your own fault, not a competitor's.

Uncollectable AR. Poor credit standards may be at fault or not enough follow up with the customer. Has it been a steady percentage? Increasing? Decreasing? It is still in your power to work this one down and make more profit in the process. Do you have someone working on the AR consistently?

Invoice stuffers. When you mail out invoices is there a collateral piece in each one offering something or notifying customers of new things? It is basically postage free since you already paid postage for the invoice. Are you doing this?

Your website. How much business are you getting through your website? What? None? Your site may still be a static display type and not interactive so customers can place orders through it. Obviously the web is how many people like to do business and your lack of updating is costing you.

Your mailing list. Needs to be supplemented by e-mail list. Direct mail outs still are effective but decision makers read their email at a higher rate than their direct mail. You are missing business if you are not working at getting email addresses from your customers. This also allows "email blasts" to them free about anything you are promoting.

Late fees/penalties. These profit drains clean up with better cash flow management.

Utilities. Have you installed computer controlled thermostats and removed every other incandescent light bulb? Put in more insulation? Aired up company tires and lined up front ends? Turned down the hot water heater temp? Turn out lights when not using them? Re-use copy paper's back side when running internal copies/prints? Buying gas at Costco? Adds up.

There Is No Fountain Of Profit

Those are easy ones but here is a harder one. Your sales manager has just come to you out of breath about how you are losing deals because your prices are higher. He is discouraged and you are concerned. "Holy cow. I guess I better get them lower prices or our competitors will have us for dinner" you are persuaded. It may consume your thoughts as you try and make a decision to lower your profit margins based upon perceptions your competition is whipping you.

You should be reassured that your competition has not found the Fountain of Profit although he may be very good at making you think it. It is important to understand what a customer considers the 'lowest price.' That would be *the vendor who best meets his needs at the lowest price.* What gets overlooked is your salesperson and his product presentation/representation just did not, in the customer's mind, satisfy the situation. That is the same thing as having a higher price to the customer. He may tell your rep he lost on 'price' to send him on his way. It is likely there was more to it. In my experience, a deal comes down to being decided on price only when a customer considers all proposals identical and there is no other factor distinguishing one vendor from another. You need to always distinguish yourself from competitors by proving you have the most meaningful benefits.

As OE we could obsess about our prices, or, decide for things more profitable than lowering prices and profitability and designing yourself out of business, such as:

More Coverage. You could decide your salespeople and manager need more training and are not at the top of their game. Maybe somebody needs to be replaced. Maybe it would be better time spent on expanding territory and hiring another rep. If successful, this will be a better move than to lower prices in the name of hopefully beating a competitor who could, in turn, lower his price even more to keep his GOOB going. (And, what to do in those price war situations? I always told my salespeople to go find another customer.)

More product. All owners crave more business and more gross profit. In addition to better sales training and more reps another way is to begin selling and servicing a new product. Find something compatible with current products and people. My company has sold copiers for 29 years but it has became a mature market with no growth and even some decline. After looking for a supplemental product I decided on a digital water cooler/purifier. It eliminates water jugs. The product brings service/supply revenue and my existing service techs can install it. It brought a new group of customers, large warehouses. It has been better than hoped for and more than makes up for losing some copiers sales to crazy competitors.

TeleMarketing. The phone is still the quickest way to reach people and get an appointment. Sure there are a lot of turn downs and voice mail but telemarketing is a pure numbers play. You just want to mine a few gold nuggets. Telemarketing and email-marketing are more important than years ago because it is harder to get into a building because of security. All salespeople need to telemarket but the power play is to hire a dedicated telemarketer who snags appointments for sales reps making them more productive than they would otherwise be.

Email marketing. You should be collecting email addresses as you go along, especially of key decision makers. These types tend to read their email if they don't do anything else. They may not always answer their phone but they will always 'see' their email although that does not mean they will open it. Attach (you do know how to attach, right?) a piece of company literature by scanning it to file and then attaching to the email. You can send a email 'blast' of the same email and attachment to your whole email list. A great appeal of email marketing is no postage expense.

Direct mail. It takes a customer seeing a product offer three times before they act on it. A good quarterly plan is to mail out postcards since there is nothing to open. Marketing pros stress that a good direct mail piece includes a mechanism to respond with such as a cut out, postage paid, reply card or at least a phone number. Emphasize a special offer.

Keeping customers/replacing customers. Did you know that at any given time 20 per cent of your customers are considering making a change that could affect your business relationship? Some are no fault of yours, some are. Customers move, close departments, go out of business, downsize, merge, get angry at you, like somebody better, upgrade to products you do not sell and so on. Change is going on constantly. The day the new phone book comes out it is 10 per cent out of date due to these same factors. Anyway, you need to be diligent in keeping existing customers. Plan to add enough new ones to counter those exiting in order to grow. By the statistics, if you did not add one new customer in five years you would be left with zero customers.

There are critical forks where you must decide what is really beating you and what is the best course of action. Are we really beating ourselves? Are we skilled enough to go toe to toe with the competition? It is both, but you do not have control over your competition, only yourself.

I have an analogy. I am a race fan. All drivers scream they need more horsepower (lower prices) to win. The chief will calm his driver and tell him there is more speed to be gained in adjusting the chassis than the engine. He explains he will add tire pressure, decrease this, increase that, adjust weight bias and so on and this will give more speed. You look to do something similar—to get more speed out of your own shop, to worry less about others, and to not depend on simple answers like lowering prices in order to win. **There are more victories to be won working out the kinks in your own operation than in beating the competition**.

Until you can say "yes, I am doing that" to all these things then you remain your biggest competitor. Worry about this more than beating the competitor nose to nose. That is not to say that is not important but if you can get competent on all the above you will be on your way to "beating the competition" more often.

Your Own Company

Your Greatest Competitor

Know the Market

Once you have a better handle on your own company you will be more of a threat to others in your market. The first priority is to determine your market—either B2B, business to business—or B2C, business to consumer. If you are B2B, marketing is more narrow and specialized. If you are B2C then every household in the city is a prospect. Each has a much different method of selling to its prospects. One uses mass media and the other doesn't.

B2B.

When your business is other businesses the best way to reach them is "feet on the street" or outside salespeople. Seminars are good too. Put on a learning type experience at a hotel or your office on a topic of general business interest. Telemarketing is heavily used in B2B to set appointments for reps. Direct mail followed up with a phone call is also effectively used. A response rate of 1%, yes one, is considered an average response from a direct mail campaign. Radio ads, targeted during "drive time" in the morning (6-8a.m.) and evening (4-6p.m.) can be effective to reach decision makers. Some local cable television may be efficient at targeting prospects.

One marketing technique I recommend is "Lunch and Learns." These are mini seminars held at your office for a handful of current customers. Lunch is served and a 45 minute product demonstration or power point is presented for discussion.

B2B businesses need to join chambers of commerce and networking groups to make useful contacts. These groups provide a mailing list of its members to contact. Good mailing lists are available on line. Info USA seems to be outstanding in this area and can sort a list for you with seemingly endless criteria. They can provide e-mail lists and have names of company managers such as the IT director. A good up to date customer list can prove invaluable and lets you shoot with a rifle instead of the shotgun approach which saves wasted mailings.   It can be worthwhile to purchase a yearly subscription to these mailing list companies that lets you access their data base whenever you want.

Our company has taken on a water cooler as an additional product. We find our best customers are large warehouses. We poke around to see what publications warehouse people read. *Inbound Logistics* magazine is one. This magazine will sell you the mailing list of its local subscribers—great prospects—if you buy advertising. We are working that angle. Another idea is to advertise on a trade association's web site or sponsor their newsletter to further target logical prospects.

B2C.

Marketing to consumers is a very large market, therefore has many more competitors, and calls for use of the mass media such as radio, TV and newspapers. A good location is also important if you are trying to sell the public. Yellow pages work. Big display ads are usually not much more effective than smaller ones. Repetition of the ad brings the best results, not the size of it. Yellow pages and mass media advertising do not work well for B2B marketing.

B2C companies are usually selling recognized brand names and the manufacturers frequently provide co-op funds and subsidize advertising efforts. Any ad you place needs to be designed by a graphic artist. Any photo needs to be taken by a professional photographer as well. These two things mean your ad will not look amateurish which may be worse than running no ad at all.

Launch Continuously

I learned a valuable lesson in getting more business or getting something to happen when nothing is: launch something, anything. Have you ever heard of a war, and running a small business is a form of combat, won without launching plenty of artillery? Generals (you) order up many rounds in hopes of a few hitting the intended target. Same for you!

It may be launching yourself into a chamber of commerce or sales/marketing group. It may be you assign a sales reps to join trade associations or chambers in outlying cities. It may be you participate in trade shows you never have. You may run ads positioning your business in a new way. Network. Take on a new product. Contact a competitor and see if he is interested in selling his business. Send a rep to a school to be trained on a new product. On and on. You are that pinball trying to stay in motion. The **Law of the Pinball** says the longer you can keep the pinball in play the greater its odds of hitting something for a big score! Lights and bells and whistles and extended playing time! *Law of the Pinball.*

Salespeople live a career of Pinball. They network and prospect. For ones that make a living at it, their efforts result in running into people who buy. A running back on a football team is a Pinball player. Here is another example, if a little unlikely. I looked in the phone book for a graphic designer to help with my book. It led me to 'way downtown' since I live in the country forty miles away. After I had put down my address, Gallaway, TN. (pop. 827) the owner said she owned 100 acres there and was developing it into a subdivision with investors. It turned out to be the 100 acres across the street from me! Since I have a farm company called 'Dirt and Destruction' that has a bulldozer, tractor, and bush hogging equipment I asked if we could do some work for her and we are.

A simple way to put this: one thing leads to another. You need to lead it. The role of the OE is to *make things happen*. For anything to happen you have to set something in motion. That is totally in your control and has nothing to do with a competitor. Absolutely you do not know if it is going to amount to anything. To do nothing is to not be doing your job. If nothing has been set in motion it is a certainty that nothing is going to happen. All marketing and promotion comes down to the Law of the Pinball.

A company hopes that by putting its message out there, keeping up its momentum, and having it run into as many people as possible its products will light up the sales charts.

The 'E' in OE could just as well stand for executive because you are supposed to be that as much as anything—one who executes courses of action. *One who gets things done.* Sometimes the problem with your business is you. You are just not doing what needs to be done. Or, you are not executing when it is time. It doesn't do any good to get a vaccination once you are ill. To what degree your lack of execution is hurting your business is for you to determine. Your failure to execute may get your business an execution.

It takes months to get things in motion in business and more months to get them done. Get them started when you don't really need them. Then you have some options when you need some. When you have free creative time say to your assistant: 'Call the rep from ABC company and tell him to come in and show me what he has. I may want to add a new product. Or, contact three new banks for me and see if they will send a commercial loan officer to talk to us about a possible new relationship.' You can always use a good sales rep so issue these directives: 'Contact Monster.com and Careerbuilder.com and get me the best rates on posting a job opening.' Same for the newspaper. You may need some promising temporary help so you load this one: 'Debe, contact the Dean of Business at the university and see if they have anybody who could benefit from an internship here this summer. While you are at it, have the Convention Center send us their schedule of events. We can see if there is one that makes sense for us to stage an exhibit.' Launch! Launch! Fire in the hole! Be proactive not reactive.

This chapter is about getting things done and sizing up weaknesses due to your fault and not a competitor's. An honest look at the state of your business operations may be painful but can only make you stronger. Business is a tough taskmaster and does not wait around for anyone.

If you find yourself stalled out, get moving by taking some small actions or delegating it to someone to get it going. In any case, if you are negligent in executing vital things and letting sloppy operations continue, then you are heading towards GOOB. You can't blame this one on the competition. Time to get it going?

Design Elements

Don't compete against yourself.   *Tighten up operations.*

Swoop, don't scoop.   *B2B or B2C?*

More profit to be gotten out of you own   *Be the Designer in Chief*

operation than your competitor's.

PART TWO:
Dealing With The Business

As a business owner you have to be a good business mechanic. You have set one big machine in motion and, at times, it wants to break down. What to do? The best practice is preventative maintenance so that the business does not lie down on you in the first place! Part Two will give you ideas on that. Even with the best periodic attention you will still suffer breakdowns. In this section you will read about techniques to use during such times, especially ones that keep you from heading out of business.

The number one problem in small business is inadequate cash flow so we need tools to deal with it. Salespeople drive your revenues but can also drive others crazy. Let's be sure we understand them. Technology is our great business friend so we will take a look at what can help us there. All business owners are in business to make a profit so getting your pricing, profit margins, and product selections right are key. There might be a lawsuit to deal with that suddenly arises.

We will examine all these things and more in Part Two of *Going Out Of Business By Design*.

Managing Trouble

*'You got trouble my friend, right here in
River City. Trouble with a capital T'*

From "The Music Man"

Owning a business has periods of great satisfaction and
punishing difficulties. My 29 years of it says there are more periods
of difficulties than satisfaction. **A lot of that will be caused by
you!** This book is about minimizing trials and tribulations or
preventing them. If you are good at dealing with trouble you
greatly advance your business longevity. If you cannot work on
heading off trouble your business will feel more like living with a
chronic illness instead of what you had in mind.

Business owners are such because they cannot work well for
others or cannot realize their potential working for others. They
are a prickly, talented, complicated, sometimes frustrating bunch.
It is even possible, dare I say, they themselves have been trouble!
OE's are driven, fueled by much more passion than most people.
Passion for one's work provides needed horsepower. This book

wants to find out if you can handle the steering wheel. Can you drive? The statistics say that 70% of you cannot. Shouldn't that make you mad?

Despite all the uncertainties and obstacles, the truth is entrepreneurs/owners don't want anything else which is both admirable and fatal. The OE has talents in some areas that are top percentile but in others the expertise needed is lower than the average Joe's. Because of that he is vulnerable to trouble, especially any outside his basic expertise. What to do? Read on.

It is a certainty the OE will have trouuuuuubllle. Might as well list it on the balance sheet, as a liability. Put it as a line item on the income statement as an expense. Trouble is your regular visitor. As CEO, **if eight out ten things brought to your attention in a day are not neutral to negative, then you are not getting the truth!** Positive points do not usually rule a day. To make matters worse, most OE's never have the resources they would like to deal with trouble. They must seemingly solve nuclear problems with fire extinguishers. It just emphasizes that the true nature of small business ownership is *combativeness*. Are you good with that?

Trouble is *normal* in business. It is not something to feel you should not have. It just is. An NFL lineman knows trouble is part of his job. He's getting wacked, sacked, piled on and incurs all manner of physical abuse. He accepts this, guards against it with pads, coaching and all the athletic ability he can develop. He takes it head on, with blocks and sacks and thus is All Pro. He is paid well and lives to play more games. He is not unlike the OE. You want to be All Pro, well paid, and play a long time.

Sad to say, though, only 31% of start ups last seven years according to the SBA. Only 44% make it four years. There is obviously a lot of trouble revealed within those statistics. These odds should be sobering. The odds of winning something in a slot machine are in the 90's. Historically, money in savings doubles every ten years. Yet here you go wanting into something with odds a Las Vegas sports bookie would decline. Why? What is going wrong here?

The most frequent cause cited for business failure is mismanagement. Some 70% of entrepreneurs get it going, have something viable, but years later—kaapoooee! The jury is in and says they make serious errors. What are they? Experience says there is a failure to deal successfully with trouble and to recognize indicators pointing to GOOB. Have your attention? You are not on this entrepreneurial journey to see it end in seven years when your child needs tuition. What is all this trouble?

Since, like me, you have a short attention span I will itemize (business people love bullet points) particularly common business troubles. These are not in any order of severity. I have put a solution with some of them.

- You are being sued. Lawyer says $275 hour, up front. *If you are being sued relax a bit. It can take more than a year for your case to come to trial if it is over $15,000 and several more years to end it. That is bad news if suing. Settling is frequently cheapest.*

- You are audited for sales tax, FUTA, SUTA, IRS, workman's comp., etc. *Do not represent yourself! Always use a representative like a CPA. Do not meet individually with the auditor.*

- A key employee quit, taking valuable customers too. *If this person was management they can be prosecuted for taking "trade secrets" and stopped. Prosecution may be worth the expense if a top "rainmaker." Not worth the expense if "average" or below.*

- You have been losing money. *See more in this chapter.*

- Inventory is not moving. *Try e/Bay or barter. It gets worth less every month you have it. Maybe rent it out.*

- Your manufacturer cannot ship it when you need it. *Go get it?*

- A major customer is
  a)leaving town
  b)bankrupt
  c)canceling you
  Normal.

- Construction is being done in front of your business. *Try talking to the mayor or city engineer.*

- Company morale is low. *See leadership chapter.*

- A new competitor now carries your same product line. *Surely another competitor is nothing new.*

- Your area of town is deteriorating. *Move. It usually seems to get worse. Keep your building leases short to leave you flexible.*

- New technology has obsoleted product. *Still need good service and instruction.*

- Some AR is uncollectible. *Establish a relationship with a collection attorney. Have a dedicated AR person. Both pay for themselves.*

- An employee has embezzled. *You may have insurance that covers this. Have fidelity bonds on people who handle money. At least $100,000.*

- You have a personal crisis. ***Stay physically fit. Morally fit. Read Matthew 7 v.19***. My wife reads this to me regularly.

- Your sales manager quit so now you are him.

- A company vehicle caused an accident.

- Cash flow is tight and things are grinding to a halt. *Cash flow is #1 business problem. See chapter on this.*

- Your identity has been stolen.

- The bank won't loan money you need. *Shop around.*

- A disgruntled salesperson gave a competitor your hot list. *The sting of this will be over in a few months.*

- Your energy and enthusiasm are waning. *Increase physical exercise. Twenty minutes daily. Increase contact with key people.*

- There has been a burglary. *You have insurance, right?*

- Your computer has crashed and valuable data lost. *A tech can still retrieve it off your hard drive.*

- Profit margins are falling. *Are you figuring them right? Prices? Cost of Goods? Expense control?*

- A physical inventory shows significant shrinkage you must write down. *Investigate if any internal theft. Otherwise, it is poor accounting practices.*

- A major supplier has put you on credit hold. *They lose too so they want to work with you.*

- Fuel, insurance, rent, tax, repair, payroll, utility, interest, phone, medical, postage, advertising costs have risen. *Raise prices.*

- Your manufacturer may cancel you if you don't sell more. *Frequently a bluff but you cannot be held hostage.*

- You have to fire someone. *If you are sure then the sooner the better.*

- You have to hire someone. *Use internet. Monster.com. Careerbuilder.com*

- You can't sell your old building. *Not helpful but don't buy buildings.*

- There is a lot of turnover in the sales department. *Hate to say it but this is normal.*

- Employee(s) have substance, financial, marital, legal problem. *Help them once and only if they cooperate.*

- Recession has decreased sales. *Take temporary measures. Recessions end.*

- The internet now sells your product cheaper than you can. *The internet does not supply service, training, location or people. You can.*

- You can't keep the quality of hire you need. *Work harder on providing more non-cash benefits.*

- I'm working 60 hours a week. *You are not delegating. You or your personal life will not last. Anything burning down there?*

These should give you some ideas. There are surely more. Some by themselves will do you in if unchecked. Of course, you will have more than one going simultaneously. The **road to success is always in disrepair**. Road Work Ahead! Are you ready to do yours?

But trouble can be your friend. It forces a look at areas we neglect. Its pressure makes us hatch better ideas. It alerts us like a dashboard light that our design needs tweaking. It provides opportunity to pull your team in and get help and input from them.

I was good at managing trouble and looked at it as a creative opportunity. I would complain about it, maybe get down about it, but then…I would get activated and my best work seemed to have come from that. I was really better at handling trouble than prosperity. In 29 years I know I felt threatened more times than General Motors at a

> *"Tell me and I will forget. Show me and I will remember. Involve me and I will understand."*
> *--Confucius*

bail out hearing. But I learned a valuable thing about why I have survived. Trouble just upped my game. Anything threatening my business was akin to a bully breaking in my back yard to threaten my child (and my independence?). I was *all in* with an internal attitude that you just will not be able to do this!

Let's make sure we know Trouble, expect it, and are willing to take it on. Let this book help keep it at bay and to *pro-actively* shut out Mr. T. To do anything less is GOOB.

Since you are now clued on trouble we will take a look at techniques to use when it arrives.

Invoke Eye of the Tiger

The first thing that needs to be done when serious trouble threatens is invoke the Eye of the Tiger. This is a mental attitude. You have seen the face of a tiger seconds away from jumping prey. The focused look of concentration and determination in his eyes commands respect and leaves no doubt that he is going to conquer his target. If you saw the *Rocky* boxing movie the theme song was "Eye of The Tiger." Rocky attained it and used it to up his focus to defeat a bigger opponent.

Two such Tiger Eyes are President Harry Truman and pilot John Sullenberg. Harry Truman was faced with ending a terrible war that was claiming a lot of lives. He decided to drop the first atomic bomb to end things. John Sullenburg was piloting a jet full of passengers when it hit a flock of birds disabling all engines. His focus became to glide the plane into a landing in the Hudson River. He did without a single casualty. Do we doubt for one minute that either of these two leaders had a face whose eyes looked just like a tiger's? More importantly, that these faces reflected undaunted determination within?

How about the man with Tiger in his name—Tiger Woods. Ever seen his face in a golf tournament, especially when he is trying to win from strokes down and usually does? He is the embodiment of concentration and determination. These are things that help make him successful. These are the same things you need when trouble strikes. They rub off on your troops and inspire them to take on a similar frame of mind putting more power to the problem solving. This is leadership.

These men are the epitome of *all in* when dealing with trouble. So it needs to be with you in crisis. Invoke Eye of the Tiger. Just do not be denied until you have conquered. Eye of the Tiger means taking a laser to anything, any thought, any "it can't be done" and vaporizing it. Procrastinators perish in this environment. Not you though, because you will be burning rocket fuel.

The most obvious trouble is financial. There is red ink because sales are low or expenses high, or both, poor cash flow, and increased competition. You will face these maybe continuously. I joke I lost a little money five months out of the year, made a little money five months out of the year, lost a lot of money one month and made a lot of money another month (total 12 months). The year's hope for profit was that the month we made a lot was bigger than the month we lost a lot. Once you reach a YTD loss of 25% of your working capital you need to take measures to stop it right there. Inadequate cash flow is the number one financial problem in small business therefore I have a separate chapter on it.

Let's look at profit issues next but remember this: **"Cash dictates what you can do today, profit says what you can do tomorrow**." Both are critical but different.

Reducing Expenses

There are numerous small reductions to scratch out and you need to do that. However, I am going to discuss a few large ones. First rule of cutting expenses: cut once, cut deep enough. Let us add: cut soon enough. The longer you wait to take the needed action then the more money is lost. Stop short of cutting company 'muscle tissue'. Once you start slashing your ability to do business, especially sales related things, it is counterproductive and points you towards GOOB. You cannot cut your way to prosperity but it can hold you in there for a time.

Cutting employees first comes to mind but you can lose valuable expertise and hit morale. **I have found that asking everyone to take a 5% temporary reduction in pay—10% maximum—is better**. It also gives immediate relief. If this does not do it *then* lay off. Going to four day weeks is another possibility. Even asking everyone to reduce by two days a month helps. You might stay away from reducing the lowest paid people. They are already stressed and may seek elsewhere if reduced.

When pay is reduced you save the pay, employer FICA contributions, and taxes tied to payroll like workman's comp. Employees save payroll taxes on that money so a $200 gross monthly cut is like $150. It may soften the blow if some can work from home during the reduction period. This saves commute time, gas, dry cleaning, car wear, and gives some freedom. A computer with software can dial them into the company's server. It may be a good idea to do this anyway and free up office space for something else. Would this help someone cut day care expense?

While these are cost measures they try to spare jobs. Employees usually see this and you win a few points amidst the gloom. Something else happens: employees dig in more when their pocketbook is touched. Maybe it is human nature. Maybe it was just the thing needed or maybe their slack caused things to get bad. Your call. New methods emerge from the clampdown and praise the hell out of anyone coming up with something better.

Have your CFO take the chart of accounts and hammer every line item. It is nuts and bolts grinding but it works. One time we found $150 a month from four dirt mat rentals. Stuff just gets by you so looking at everything produces surprising things. Challenge all employees to look for things and bonus them if they find savings.

Next, as owner, take a loan from the company instead of a paycheck. It is still cash out but the loan does not hit the bottom line as a paycheck will. If you get $10,000 monthly then a loan to you for that amount "saves" $10,000 that month as well as payroll taxes on it. You must pay the company back with interest. You don't have to pay it back actually, but if you do not you then have to declare it as pay and pay taxes on it. The best way to do this, providing your company can spare the cash, is to pay it back with a low payment over a number of years which increases personal cash flow.

Another profit reducer is in the cost of goods sold. Grind on suppliers, especially larger ones. Show them continued loyalty for any help once on better footing. Demand lower prices, free shipping, bonus product, whatever, to affect reductions in this category.

Through all hard times do your best to maintain your personal credit score. It seems lenders look at your FICO score for creditworthiness as much as anything. There really is no "credit score" on your small business other than a D&B report, if you report, so lenders look at owners' personal to get some idea. You can run into trouble with your personal credit score with business obligations getting on it. They are not supposed to be there. All small business owners have to personally guarantee company debt and obligation but it is not supposed to end up on your personal credit score since these things are not paid from personal income. But they do. Subchapter 'S' corporations would be an exception to this.

When I went to buy my second home years ago the lender said I could not possibly afford the payments. Incredulous, I asked why? You have nearly $600,000 in various debts that would consume too much of your income. It took a while but once they saw it was company debt everything went through fine. Recently, I had nine company car payments showing up on my personal credit that shouldn't. Here we go again.

It seems it only takes a nanosecond for a negative thing to hit your credit score but takes an ice age to pass before you can get them off if they do not belong.

Best to have your lending friends get the full credit report on you in order to get the whole story and not just your score. Show proof that things are not paid with personal funds that end up on your personal report. Get your banker to go over your credit report and tell you how he views it.

Increasing Revenue

Running red may signal you are not charging enough. Time to raise prices? If you have not in three years you are in line for a 15% increase. Every new dollar raised and accepted by your customer goes to the bottom line. If a customer comes unglued over an increase, and a few do, don't fight it. Just put it back where it was.

You can benefit from adding itemized, add on charges to invoices. Do you add a finance charge for late pay? Are you charging for mileage or drive time? Are disposal charges appropriate for hazardous materials? Extra charges for having to take your product up stairs? After hours charges? Fuel surcharge? MPS charge (misc. parts & supplies, oils, rags, cleaners)? Customer abuse (of machine not you) charge? Phone support time? New operator training? "Move you to first in line" charge?

I do not mean to sound pinch penny. These are all legitimate charges. They are for something extra provided to the customer. It is just that you may never have thought of it like that, or done them free. This may be why you are red. These all add important profit. If you look at invoices today, from a credit card company to a tire change, to a bank statement, you will see much the same. These charges are likely being charged to you. If so, you are just covering your expenses. As part of this examination process, banish the word "free" from your vocabulary too.

Revenue problems are helped by taking on a new product compatible with your company's ability. **Selling more things to existing customers is one of the best way to boost revenues.** Our primary business is office machines but we added a jugless water cooler. It was on display at a convention. I signed on. We do well with it and each sale is added gross profit. It is another office product we could return to our customer to talk about if they were not in the market for anything else.

If sales are down then so is working capital. You need inexpensive ways to increase company and product exposure. Target networking groups and business associations in your city. Assign yourself and salespeople to join one to begin a networking campaign. Another technique is to ask good prospects if they will "evaluate" a new product you are thinking of offering. Put stuff in companies for 30 days and see what happens. If you have a public facility put things on display more, make them more visible and put them outside. They can't buy it if they can't see it. See if you can display a product at a mall or another company.

Have an open house. Get out your customer list and mail an invitation followed with a phone call. Have all your products on full display with clear to understand information next to them. Drive your sales force harder. Have a "blitz" week with monetary prizes for most calls and appointments set. Post special offers on your website. Try to get an article written about your business by local papers. Send out a press release. It may help.

A good book to get for inexpensive ways to market is *Guerrilla Marketing*.

Suffice it to say that downturns call for extra effort from everyone. There should be an increase in shoe leather burned and holes in soles should appear. For fun, have a "sole check" one day and award a prize to the person(s) with any holes in their shoe sole.

Buying a company can boost revenues, expertise, and critical mass quicker than anything. An acquisition is about buying positive cash flow and increasing your base. Stick with a competitor in your field. Feel out the owner directly and look for one wanting to get out. He needs to stay six months but no longer. Two owners never get along.

Acquisitions typically involve about half of the purchase price down and the rest in owner financing. The total debt service from the deal needs to be covered by the new cash flow from the combined companies' economies. One company needs to move in with the other. This eliminates duplicate expenses which frees up new cash flow which increases your selling price. On top of this there needs to be additional positive cash flow left over for you. **The formula for a good acquisition is one + one must =3.** In other words, the two companies together must generate more positive cash flow than the two separately or you should not do it. Or, at the least, not pay anything for it. You do not have to be Donald Trump to complete an acquisition. You do have to audit the company's books, make sure the businesses are compatible, and retain most of the employees. An acquisition can make it a whole new ballgame for you.

I have a friend who has a retail store and I really admire his thought process to increase business. He tries to schedule free events in front of his store to attract customers. This can be a car wash for high school kids raising money, letting Girl Scouts sell cookies or the Salvation Army ring the bell. This is all free to him and drives more traffic. *Recycle your old computer here!* Good thinking.

Containing Employee Issues

This is a broad category and its issues include hiring, firing, embezzlement, turnover, morale and performance problems.

Most issues that lead to employee trouble are preventable with good proactive management. That is where your work lies. Once an employee has embezzled, continually underperformed, or has quit, it is over anyway.

You should enjoy this work. To me, employees are the greatest source of enjoyment in operating a small business. I have a saying: "The thing that makes people the happiest is people." If you tie your feel goods to statistical data you will be unhappy more months out of the year than not. Numbers are up and down but people are more reliable and certainly more fun.

All answers to preventing employee problems are contained in your leadership principles, the values you lay down, and how you enforce them. Everything I know about people and handling them is in the "How Am I Leading" chapter. Those things have proved true for me and are something I am particularly pleased about learning. Other than that, I just emphasize again, be compassionate with employees and their issues. It is the best policy. Give time, give guidance, give second chances but then move on if people still insist on sowing trouble.

Embezzlement

This is one of the worst of headaches. This is a migraine. This is serious trouble. It happens more than one would like to think. My church bookkeeper managed to get $150,000 before she was caught. My office equipment company had $30,000 of inventory taken. My Kawasaki dealership had $35,000 embezzled. I personally know three other business owners in my city that had embezzlements by their bookkeepers for these kinds of sums. The City of Memphis found an employee that got hundreds of thousands before caught.

People that embezzle are very, very good at it. It is hard to catch them in the act. You just discover it. Needless to say, this can be very damaging to your company if you cannot recover the goods. There is the added cost to you personally and business wise because it is all you can think about for weeks. The good news is there is insurance for this and you need to make sure you have it. You do have to prove the theft to the insurance company so someone with accounting expertise will have to construct a paper trail to prove the embezzlement. Insurance companies require a police report as well. I recovered the $35,000 taken at my Kawasaki dealership on insurance but not the inventory taken from e/Doc Systems.

Another shade of embezzlement is by rogue employees making side deals that management is not aware. A salesperson can type a letter on company letterhead modifying a contract. The owner is not aware of it but later gets stuck. An example is an early termination provision. Anyone who has access to company product could skillfully steal some and sell it. This shows up when a physical inventory is taken so do take one yearly to see if you have inventory 'shrinkage.'

An unscrupulous salesperson could be selling another brand 'on the side' at your company's expense. It is a good idea to have your salespeople under non-compete agreements that allow you to prosecute if necessary. To be enforceable, the OE has to give actual payment to the rep for agreeing to the terms of the contract. This makes it much more enforceable in court.

You

You are the key to it all. To be the head trouble manager (not maker) you need to manage yourself well. What is your plan for yourself? **Since you are the company's most valuable asset you need to take care of yourself like other assets**. Remember all that debt you personally guarantee! Keep yourself well insured, maintained, trained, protected, and don't abuse! Managing trouble depletes the precious rocket fuel of the OE. If there is too much trouble or depletion it can shut down the owner. The OE needs to delegate as much as possible. His warriors really need to step things up if need be to help preserve the OE as a valuable asset.

Your energy level and creative levels have to be significantly higher than the average bear. What is your Motion Quotient? (see illustration). You need to have a Red Bull brain but don't drink the stuff. The yearly wear and tear on an OE is higher than most jobs. If a dog year equals seven human years then an OE year equals about one and a half regular human years.

You must have an above average ability to handle stress. It will take all this just to stay even. I start with physical fitness. You cannot do your best in this role without it. Keeping fit, especially with cardio work, keeps the brain performing its best. You will make better decisions. It keeps mood and energy higher. It negates stress. To neglect this is to admit you are not willing to do your best. Devote one hour every other day to fitness. Postpone things that get in the way of your workout, not the other way around. I say working out boosts your business IQ by 20 per cent.

Manage for stress by cutting yourself slack in little things. I avoided traffic in the morning and afternoon by arriving at 9:00 and leaving at 4:00. Do not work a zillion hours a week. This means you are failing as a manager. Use your lunch hour to have a pleasurable work/eat session with managers. Learn to delegate well. Do not take everything onto yourself. Have an assistant do all that you do not want to do not have time to do.

The company is going to move at the speed you do. When you are slowing down, find out why, and adjust. Delegating headaches to a speedier person works. It is important for you to feel good and upbeat most of the time. It signals employee morale and a feeling of security so pay attention to it. This is not being selfish! You are the radar. The responsibility of a business can be all consuming in both good times and bad. It can consume marriages and families. This is not being successful! For some, owning a business becomes a genuine addiction and does what all addictions do—destroy something. You need to balance with outside activities and family time. These are cushions and needed maintenance for you. Use your faith as well and for sure, don't let it succumb! All this will go a long way to preventing burnout. If you burnout, what do you think is going to happen to your company?

As the chief firefighter of the place you also need to know when to speak up to your troops. I let my employees know where we stand each month—whether we made a profit or a loss. Let them know! It is just the score of the ballgame. If it is a negative number they will dig a little deeper and try a little harder. This may be just what you need. Many owners are reluctant to give out financial data, especially if it is negative, for fear of 'how it might look'. Silly. That is like the scorekeeper at a ball game removing the home team's score if it is behind.

Hold a formal meeting and use your financial statements as a guide for discussion. "We have too much inventory. Our 90 day AR is too high. Our vehicle repair bill has caused us to lose money this month. We lost a few customers last month so our revenue is down. " Whatever it is. Employees really, really appreciate the honesty and integrity of your effort. They become better business people in the process. It is just human to do a more effective job if you know what the circumstances are. So get rid of any 'this would not look good' worries because that will just make it worse, not help you manage your trouble, and may lead to GOOB. All small businesses look bad some of the time. Maybe most of the time. They are not going to have the profile of a Fortune 500 company so do not pretend you should. Your competitors fight the same stuff so get a leg up on them by making your troops better educated and better informed.

All OE's will do well to take the same Hippocratic Oath doctors do, at least the famous line: "First, do no harm." Realize *when* you are weak and try to avoid making major decisions then. Realize *where* you are weak and improve yourself there. Doing both will help reduce the trouble that originates with you.

Real Estate

Occupancy costs are among your highest expenses. You are either leasing or buying. It is probably better to lease than to buy a building. Most large companies lease but could buy. Why?

When a OE thinks about real estate it is usually in relation to a home. Homes almost always appreciate and resell. You might expect the same from a building. Commercial real estate is different. Homes and buildings are both real estate like a golf ball and football are both balls. Commercial buildings do not always appreciate and many times never re-sell at all. Look around town. You will not see many vacant homes but you will buildings.

You can pay on a building a long time, carry it on your financials for hundreds of thousands of dollars, and when it comes time to re-sell find it worth zero. Yes zero. Commercial buildings are frequently occupied for their proximity to commerce such as a mall, a plant, hospital, neighborhood etc. These things change and can run down to even slum status over time. Certain areas of town which were once commercially hot turn cold. This is how it is with real estate.

There is another problem. Say you are in a decent area and have outgrown your building. You get excited, plan a new one and are sure you will sell your old one since it is in a "good" area. To do this you have to start building your new building before you sell your old one. This is risky. It can take a long time to sell—maybe two years. While you are in your new building, you are still making payments on your old building, plus property taxes, plus insurance, plus utilities, and landscaping—expensive. This kind of doubling of costs can ruin your balance sheet.

Too Little or Too Much?

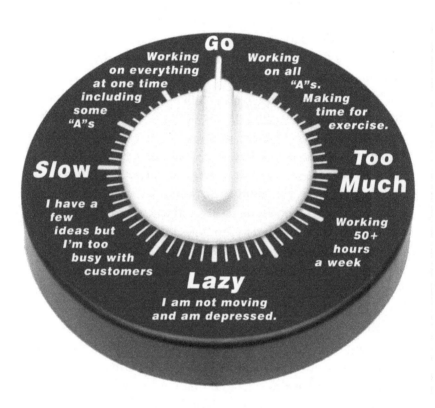

Motion Quotient

Maybe you try not building your new one until you sell your old one. This is difficult, as well, since it takes maybe six months or more to get the new one built. Your buyer may not go with this and you lose the sale. The buyer will also want your old building redesigned since most buildings do not suit the new tenant as is. At the least, you are paying for two buildings for a while and this is expensive. Moving expenses also need to be considered in all cases.

Lastly, if your business does sell you still own the building and must continue to pay the upkeep until it sells or rents. If you want to sell your business owning the building could prove a big obstacle.

The problem with buying a building is that it is a transaction that takes a long term asset of 20 or 30 years and tries to make it a compatible match with a business segment that has a 70% failure rate in seven years.

Leasing avoids the possibility of ruining your balance sheet. You can frequently get free rent (six months?) to cover moving expenses. If you need more space it is usually available in the same office park. Do not lease without the assistance of a tenant representative. These are agents who represent you and are paid by the landlord to get you as a tenant. Tenant reps do not cost you anything and will save you a lot. Do you know how to work through expense stop language, for example? Didn't think so. Tenant reps know where all the empty space is in town and the best deals.

If you are going to build do so in the very best part of town with a building someone else can re-use. This gives you the best chance for appreciation and resale.

You can cut occupancy expenses by setting up workers at home if appropriate. Another office to lose might be your own. This is probably not for everyone. I have always had a nice office but never in it much. I hop around and am in everyone else's. I like to work in our conference room since it has a big table, office equipment etc. In our current building I just left my office out and when I go in, I work in the conference room.

There is Always Something That Can Be Done

The OE frame of mind when there is trouble has to be that there is always something that can be done. Because there is. It may not seem true. You may not see a way at the moment, but you can find solutions. It may be that you need to find answers by asking others. If conditions are severe then you have to get out of the box and think creatively. It may be that to get the help you have to swallow some pride. The pursuit of the solutions will be uncomfortable but this should not matter if you can close in on what is needed.

> ➤ I had a large contract with Federal Express for about 75 machines. A large manufacturer came in at prices I could not match so FedEx cancelled us. I told the manager I had a contract for another 11 months. he said "no way." I then took it to the next level. He backed his manager. I then got to a vice president who said he would have to give it to a higher level. I got to him after a month and he told me I probably had a case and let see what he could do. Weeks later he said I would get my eleven months because he was having the incoming vendor pay it. Yeah! That bought time I needed. So you just keep driving. But I was still in a lot of trouble. I needed to replace the $35,000 monthly cash flow. I wanted to find a leveraged buyout of a competitor—no easy thing. I called on all the owners I could get to talk and eventually bought the service department of another dealer. It did what I needed to do. The loss of the Federal Express account actually helped me grow my business! As it turned out, this turning Tom's Last Stand into Strike Up the Band is what, a judge told me, won me the Memphis Business Journal's Small Business Executive of the Year in 1994. So, keep clanging. Keep banging. Law of the Pinball.

> ➤ We have ten service vehicles and during a down period I decided to trade five because the manufacturer had a $4000

rebate going. I could have reduced the purchase price but took the cash, $20,000, which went to the bottom line that month which was great. I like cash in hand better than spread over 60 months. Easy profit without even selling anything!

➤ Our lease expired during a downturn in commercial real estate. I contacted my tenant rep and began looking. Normally, we enter a seven year lease on a new building, build it out and get free rent to cover moving costs. The rep said if we wanted an empty space, somewhat "out of the way, not new, that had just been vacated by a major tenant" we could get 10 months free. The space was OK but not our usual standard. But, free rent, at $6000 at month can add up. I needed to help my bottom line so asked for *eighteen months free rent* that they could add into the back of the lease for eight years total. They did it! What a boost to that years bottom line. Way out of the box. It would take the sale of nearly $800,000 to net that same bottom line.

Playing Hardball

Maybe five per cent of the time handling trouble comes to playing hardball. You need your inner Bruce Lee. It could be that some payment out of all expectation is suddenly demanded by a taxing body or from a lawsuit. Maybe an important customer wants to terminate a contract early. We are talking large amounts here that you feel are unjust as well as very damaging to your company's well being. You must do all you can here rather than hand over way too valuable company working capital because something is trying to intimidate you. You will have to have power behind it. Or, at least the perception of it.

Federal Express is headquartered in our city and the new Congress is trying to pass a law making it easier for unions to organize FedEx's 300,000 workers (go figure). Anyway, this is a real threat to the company because a union can strike which would absolutely damage the company's ability to operate much less its image. Fred Smith, CEO, wrote Congress. He said if they continued he was cancelling all orders with American company Boeing worth nearly 7 billion dollars and buying elsewhere. Hardball.

We are all small fries compared to that. What are our big power moves besides withholding our money? First of all is yourself. Put in all that passion and energy that got you a company. Make your voice loud, persistent and demanding. Have supporting documents. Go up the chains of command. Have your attorney do something. Go to your congressman's office for help too. You may have to solicit support from interest groups or business associations or peers. Don't take "no" for an answer. Establish beyond a doubt that the other side has a fight on their hands. Let them know they will have to work very hard to get this money. Once they are *convinced* of this it may bring a settlement. Most know a fight takes a long time to settle. Your opposition may not want that.

The Law of the Pinball is good to keep in mind when dealing with trouble. Try to keep yourself in play long enough, with all manner of body English, contortion, reflexes and keen eyesight and eventually you will hit something that lights for a score.

Winning Ugly

In very tough times like these it may come down to winning ugly. You may have to resort to unpleasant strategies to recover your bottom line. Yes, they are ugly as neither you nor the one on the receiving end will like the way these look, but this is about survival. Here are things you can do to 'win ugly.'

- Renegotiate leases and loans. Ask your landlord and lenders to refinance your balances to a longer and lower amortization. If they won't, do it for them and tell them this is what you can do. It is likely they will live with it but also unlikely you will get anything more from them in the future.

- Deduct ten or twenty per cent from vendor invoices you have in hand. Again, if the customer wants your business he will probably live with it.

- Barter. Pay invoices from inventory you have on hand. Maybe you do free landscaping in return for some free rent. This saves cash.

- Take out pay in the form of a loan. This keeps it from hitting the bottom line as well as not having to pay payroll taxes on it. You must pay this back over time though or it will become taxable income. Take 12 to 24 months to repay.

- Be cheap. Take out every other light bulb. Decrease insurance coverage to bare bones. Cell phones to local service only etc. etc.

You do what you have to do.

Hire a Consultant

When you have too much trouble, or do not really know what to do, seek help from those who do. This can be another business owner, a businessperson's organization, or hire a consultant. A well known volunteer group that does not charge is SCORE, the Service Corp of Retired Executives. Paid consultants are a good idea. You will get more thorough help going this route. There is a right way and a wrong way to retain a consultant.

The only way you should do this is on a month to month basis with each month paid in advance. The fee might be a low of $1000 and a high of $2,000. It works out to about $100 an hour for the time you will receive. Under no circumstance hire a group that comes in with multiple consultants, stays a few weeks, gives recommendations, and then wants a large fee. Whoever you hire you will want to see a resume. As a practical matter, they should be at least 40 years old to have "been there." A good consultant should provide enough value to pay for himself.

A national consulting company that works the way I have recommended is Institute for Independent Business. There web is www. iib.org. They should have people in your area.

A good consultant should be respectful and look at you as a peer. He will need to be provided a lot of company information. Then he will spend time studying your needs and make recommendations. It can be a really comforting thing just to have a knowledgeable person to discuss matters with you. Owners are usually stingy with telling anyone what is really going on and keep a lot to themselves (died in pride?). In the process, the lens they are using to view the world becomes distorted. Their judgment can get impaired and forward motion slow to a halt. None of this is helpful.

Don't just stiff the chin and go it alone. It is not necessary nor is it smart. Be a help-seeking missile and find some help. It is out there. You get the idea here. Think large when it comes to helping yourself and what would help you. Then drive hard and you may be surprised. It is a certainty that if you do not ask, move, network, demand, and think, nothing will happen. As long as you are keeping things in play, moving until something you hit lights up, letting one thing lead to another thing, you have a good chance of diminishing your trouble. Law of the Pinball.

Design Elements

Do not run from or deny trouble.	*Identify the trouble that you are causing.*
Do not neglect physical fitness.	*Do not fire.*
	Reduce hours or pay.
Quit giving it away.	*Play hardball. Play pinball.*
Don't buy the building.	*There is always something that can be done.*

Salespeople
Nothing happens until somebody sells something

There is no more difficult person to manage than a salesperson. There is no more valuable person to your organization than a salesperson. There are few braver employees in business than a salesperson. There are no employees more insecure in business than a salesperson. There are few jobs that deal with more uncertainty than a salesperson. There are few jobs that, on average, pay as well as a salesperson. Managing all this into a smooth running sales department is about as easy as shoveling smoke.

A good salesperson is among a business's most valuable possessions. "Nothing happens until somebody sells something" goes the dictum. Think how much commerce would cease if all salespeople went on strike for a week! Good salespeople are to be heavily recognized and recruited. Take care of them like Derby Thoroughbreds because they are to your business.

I was fortunate to be trained by IBM, the best sales training around along with Xerox. We spent two months in the office and one month away in a sales school/dormitory to learn. IBM revered good salespeople. I do emphasize the word "good". A salesperson's performance was tracked like planes in the sky and frequently noted. IBM taught you how to dress as if you owned the company. Recognition is craved by salespeople. IBM knew this and showered good reps with it. I once won a trip for two to Bermuda along with a gold clock worth $1000. There were a lot of trips.

Salespeople are the athletes of the business world. They must be in a high state of physical and mental fitness, be self starters, and perform at a high level amidst uncertainty and brutal competition. The best salespeople stay physically conditioned. I hate to say this but the truth is I have never seen a "chubby" salesperson who is that successful. The pickings can be slim. There are probably more standing job openings for salespeople than for any other profession.

The best salespeople are well paid, usually six figures. As it should be since they bring in the money. A traveling salesman is paid a 25% premium to compensate for overnights and time away from home. A good salesperson is usually "free" in that he is paid out of profit he brings in. Sales work is some of the most difficult because the salesperson must find the work. In other occupations, the work finds you. A salesperson is basically unemployed at the start of each month. There is always a job opening for someone who can sell, though. A real salesperson is never without a job long.

Salespeople's Quirks

Enthusiasm is the rocket fuel in salespeople's tanks. This is what makes them extraordinary. They manage to have it while living a more negative day than most. The sales rep hears numerous "no"s while living happily on those few "yes's" each month. Owners need to see to it that this valuable propellant is preserved among their sales force. This is what is going on at all those recognition events and "pep rallies" in sales departments. A motivational speaker once said that the best example of enthusiasm is a house dog. Every time the doorbell rings he dashes wildly to answer it but it is never for him.

If a salesperson is gold then a great sales manager is Fort Knox. Managing salespeople is a little like policing Iraq. The salesperson is pounding the pavement with his weapons and encountering all kinds of opposition. He needs his door to door skills to keep him alive like a soldier. Some days it is one bomb after another. "Incoming" is what he hears all too often. For all these reasons the sales occupation claims more than its share of casualties. The sales manager who can handle all the flak could probably interchange with an Army Captain and do a decent job. He would feel right at home.

Most salespeople secretly feel they should be running the company and that those who do are one fry short of a happy meal. It is just a part of keeping themselves where they need to be: feeling superior. This is why the smart OE showers the (performing) sales rep with recognition, plaques, ceremonial prizes, raises and maybe a company car. It is appropriate because they really grow the company. Good salespeople are a bit like, oh my God, business owners. That being said, they usually lack the patience, accounting knowledge, big picture knowledge, and other knowledge that goes with ownership. They need to be reminded of this.

It is a great mistake to be annoyed by salespeople. The company that embraces salespeople as the stars of the business does best. But, of course, salespeople can be their own worst enemies with out of bounds egos, short attention spans, and poor admin skills that convey an uncaring attitude. Usually, salespeople feel admin people are "out to get them." It is not true but the reason for this feeling is their own fault. If they fill out paperwork correctly and timely that feeling vanishes. Let me say, though, that a sales rep may truly not be capable of this. It just might be that the best course is to assign help with it so he can do what he does best, bring in business. That being said, non salespeople do want to write the book *Salespeople Are From Somewhere and We From Somewhere Else.*

I could not do paperwork. I still cannot and hate it. Yet I own the business. So there is room for paperwork challenged people. The second admission is that I have never had a file cabinet with anything in it. I have never filed anything. What is the deal? Well, two wonderful people assist me in that. Please envy me. *I am valuable to my operation even though I cannot do detail* but I *am hard at work on my "A"s!* This is not the subject of this chapter but it speaks to the importance of designing the business around the traits of the owner instead of the other way around—an important thing mentioned somewhere in this book.

"I", three time Salesperson of the Year and one time IBM National Director, was called into the branch manager's office once for a serious meeting. He received complaints that I did not take enough time to instruct on customers' typewriters.

" This is IBM, Tom, and if you do not take time to instruct properly, fill out install sheets, and keep from getting customers angry, you will lose your job." He came around the desk and sat next to me. "Grip the edge of this desk with me Tom", he said. Hold tight until your fingers turn white." He wanted me to do this when tempted to leave the customer too quickly. "If you do that, maybe you can keep your job." Wow. I thought I was invincible with my record but that was IBM. The deal was you were a rounded dude. **You could sell, instruct, dress well, keep good attitude, represent the company image, and do your paperwork. It was not just that you could sell**. Boy, that is a great job description right there for any salesperson.

A major success component of a sales rep is maximizing time spent with customers or prospects and minimizing it spent elsewhere. More of this brings more sales and more money for all. Time management can be a challenge for salespeople. I direct mine to be at their first call at 9:00 and take lunch from 11:30-1. Back in the field from 1:00 to 4:30 and then in the office to do paperwork etc. I also feel proposals and number crunching needs to be done at home. The sales hours are "game time" and about the only time someone will see you. It is not a time to be in the locker room.

It is important to direct and incent your salespeople to secure new customers. We pay more commission on a net new account than an existing one. Existing customers are there frequently due to some other former rep's work or the company's work. It is easier for a rep to work them. They certainly need to be worked and retained but not at the expense of new accounts. Your customer base will decline over time if new accounts are not added regularly. A broad base of smaller accounts is an important goal because this adds stability. As a rule you do not want more than ten per cent of your revenue to come from any one account. Too much revenue tied up in a few large accounts makes you very vulnerable to any changes in them. We know change is a given in business.

An organized telemarketing effort is good use of office time. You can cover a lot of ground. To be effective telemarketing needs to be worked from a good prospect list complete with phone numbers. These can be purchased from Sales Genie or Info USA. Setting as many phone appointments as possible is important since tighter security makes it harder to get into companies today than a few years ago.

It is vital that all the customer information that sales reps gather be put into contact management software (CRM) such as Goldmine or Telemagic. This way, valuable money and time spent by your company learning a customer's particulars does not go down the drain if he leaves. It is the property of the company. And turnover is higher in sales than anywhere else. CRM software tracks contract expirations, emails, competitive installations, contacts, phone numbers etc.

It is helpful to remember that much of the time sales reps are not in control. The customer is. The customer wants it yesterday, in a different color than is in stock, will not pay until such and such is working, wants a lower interest rate etc. The rep has to return to the office and relay customer demands in the best possible way. He is really the customer advocate but the stuff he is asking for may seem overbearing. Best to go with the sales rep. He is closest to the customer and success in business means being close to the customer.

I would stress that, no matter the circumstances a salesperson faces—inventory availability, customer contact, service or repair status, AR status of a current customer, promised delivery dates, billing particulars—he is the point person for all of it. He must take responsibility for those things taking place as they should when they should. There can be great arguments between a rep and the supporting cast over who did not do what. Billing is supposed to bill it this way, delivery is to be on this day, this feature is to be installed on it, and so on. **The sales rep is to see that all this has been done according to what the customer wants and how he wants it. Nobody else.** If nothing else, it only makes sense for his income. If he does not get the sale the rep gets zero whereas all the other supporters continue to get paid. So reps, give up the arguments and guide the whole picture.

The big payoff for a sales rep comes after a few years staying in the same place. Reps who jump around rarely come to much. After three years two things have happened: you have learned your craft and have repeat customers. As time goes on you get even more repeat customers. This takes stress out of the job and helps increase income. You can make a good living selling just about anything if you commit to getting very good at it as well as forming relationships with customers. This sews the seeds for repeat business.

Sometimes the OE is torn between the idea of employing two rookie sales reps versus one senior. Both have their advantages and disadvantages. Rookies have seemingly more energy and make more calls than a senior. The question is, are those calls penetrating enough to be fruitful? The rookie rep has a harder time getting the customer to engage.

Senior reps can slow down and get a little lazy. They can begin to 'cherry pick' deals and not prospect as well as they should. However, seniors are usually much better than rookies at making profitable sales and overcoming objections that would stall a rookie. I have no conclusion here. The only helpful analogy I can think of is Yogi Berra's comment that 'When you come to a fork in the road you should take it.'

Sales and salesmanship are two of the most written about subjects in business. There are no shortage of books, columns, DVD's and blogs on selling. The reason there is so much written is a testament to the number of buyers, of course. Most are salespeople and I suggest they are one of the pillars our economy is built upon. Sales is one of the loneliest of business positions, especially a traveling rep. This is another reason there are so many books on salesmanship. The trucking industry likes to say that America's needs move by truck. But who fills those trucks? Salespeople. If all salespeople were to go on strike the economy would grind to a halt faster than a banker cashing a TARP check.

Hiring salespeople may be one of the OE's greatest headaches. It can take as much as six months to know if you have made a good hire but you should know before then. If you have not hired well then it has been an expensive six months. Sales has been my career and I learned things about who to hire and what to look for in a salesperson.

What Makes a Good One

The number one quality to have is energy. Salespeople need to be Energizer Bunnies on the job so this requires people with weapons grade go power. IBM liked to hire ex-athletes figuring they had energy and were competitive. Their other favorite category was ex-school teachers thinking they could explain products and their benefits well. Whoever you hire look for physical fitness.

A rep with a sense of urgency is highly desirable. Those with this characteristic always use the time available to best use. Time to them is the currency of their craft. For these reps there is not enough time in the day to call on everyone they wanted to. Business people with a high sense of urgency look for reasons why something can be done, and done soon, rather than why it cannot. They get upset when the customer's install takes too long or when they themselves take too long on anything.

Another quality I like to see is a quick mind. This is hard to define but those who are fast with figures, sizing up people, can 'change gears' quickly, multi-tasking types, can memorize things, get the gist of a new product quickly and the like. I knew an IBM sales manager who liked to ask the prospect to "drive him to the dry cleaners to pick up some suits". He would then say he forgot he had an appointment at the office and please get him back quickly. In the process he would watch how the prospect drove looking for quick maneuvers, fast thinking and such. His theory was that if the guy had a red car that was a good sign of an aggressive personality.

I hate to say this but I think women are a better bet than men. They are better listeners and many decision makers are men. The problem with men is that they compete with each other whether it is apparent or not. On job interviews they can come across as NFL free agents. This posture can get in the way in a sales call and does. Women could care less about this stuff. There is more of a natural conversation zone between a man and a woman which would be a helpful thing in a sales call. You are familiar with the book *Men Are From Mars and Women From Venus*.

When I began I put a big ad in the paper looking for 'IBM type' salespeople. One lady applied who had not worked in six months due to a nervous breakdown from a bad divorce. She did not dress well either and I sought to wrap the interview in a hurry.

She called back and I said I would 'get back with her' but never would. She would drop by the office hoping to catch me which happened a couple of times but I offered no encouragement. This went on until Della had called on me five times asking for this job. Finally I said to myself that you just cannot teach that kind of determination and persistence. No matter the other shortcomings, I 'gave her a chance'. We worked on things. In ten years she was my best salesperson ever, became Vice-President and was my partner in the Kawasaki dealership.

I came up with a 'talent test' that revealed a lot. I would ask the prospective hire to take a survey form I had made. It asked companies what they had for office equipment, what brands, how they liked it etc. It was just a survey with no sales element. I would ask the prospect to take a zip code or two and see how many of these he could get filled out in four hours. You could tell a lot from the number of calls, the surveys filled out, the amount of detail in them and if the person could make 'cold calls.' The top I ever got was 20. A low was six. You would hire the 20 of course and not the 6. It worked as well as anything.

Paying salespeople is an inexact science but one thing is certain—it needs to be based upon the gross profit they generate and not revenue. Otherwise, you will find the discounting salespeople do will be much higher. "But boss, I brought in $15,000 for you!" "Maybe so, Jake, but $14,000 of it went to the manufacturer and the rest to you and none to the company!" Salary should make up about 40% of expected earnings and commission 60%. If a salesperson is underperforming reduce the salary and simultaneously increase the commission. Put more of the burden on the salesperson where it belongs. If the sales are made then the pay works out the same as when the salary was higher. Bonuses can be given to drive specific needs such as getting rid of too much of a certain model. Of course, reps are not paid until the money comes in.

Design Elements

Nothing happens until something sells.   *Salespeople valuable asset.*
Reps not always in control of customer.   *Hardest people to manage.*
Toughest job in business.   *Need help with detail.*
Six figure pay common.   *Protect their rocket fuel.*

Products and Prices
When the price is not right

In my opinion, the single most serious design flaw in small businesses is in **pricing. It is invariably too low**. Ask an owner what they charge and you hear: "We try to set a fair price" We try to net $500 out of most deals." "We mark it up 35%" Why 35%? It's just what we do." "We charge whatever the market will bear." "We try to get a little below the competition." "We charge whatever it takes to get the deal." Might as well say "We believe in the price fairy." Might as well say "I really do not know how to set the price."

Answers like these reveal misunderstanding of what should go into prices. This kind of thinking can destroy bottom lines. What they reveal is a not too untypical gunslinger/macho attitude based upon "winning". But if what you have won is a deal that loses money, you have not won anything. Sometimes I hear salespeople whining about losing a deal. "How much gross profit margin was in it?, " I would ask. "Not much--15%" was the response. " Well, you didn't lose much then did you"? I reply.

Selling on price is not what professional sales is about. If it was I could send my receptionist out in a taxi cab to deliver 'The Quote'. It is about finding needs in a business and satisfying their problems. This is why you hear the word 'solutions' used so often when selling products or services to business. For a time, not a long time, some competitors can give you fits as they embark on a lowball price program. Lasting businesses are not built this way. Those doing such regularly are GOOBers and are trying to overcome the laws of business physics. They cannot be everywhere, in on every deal, so move on to the next prospect.

Setting the Right Prices

The true cost to a company for a product goes beyond its wholesale price. Selling a product through a company requires employees to receive, pack, ship, inventory, keep temperature controlled, be invoiced, taxed, insured etc. Total those things, prorated among all the product sold that year, and you have the *true cost* of a product, or labor hour. The amount added to a product's actual cost, or on top of a labor hour's actual cost, to account for the product's share or labor's share of the rest of the general overhead burden, is called **the burden rate**. The burden rate is then added to actual cost to arrive at a product's true cost to its company. All prices need to be figured based upon it as actual cost instead of using the actual hard cost itself. This is usually referred to as 'cost of goods sold.' Figure yours and never sell below it. Otherwise, you are not using true cost as the true cost. The next time you are asked about your pricing a great answer would be: "We get 35% above our burden rate." Wow.

This brings us to the term **hurdle rate**. This is the amount of return on investment that an owner or investor considers the minimum acceptable amount of return (his hurdle), on what is invested. In our case here, our investment can be thought of as our actual cost plus burden rate of an hour of labor or the price of a product, as I detailed. So the owner needs to set his hurdle rate to establish what he will accept as the *lowest* price a product or labor hour will be. It would not be unusual to charge more.

You frequently hear business people say something to the effect that "at least we made something on it" as a rational for selling something too cheaply. Thus if the product costs $700 and it sells for $775, you may hear that response. It is not an accurate one. The best statement to make for this type of sale is "that sale returned a negative ROI (return on investment). After adding in all the company time and assets that this sale encumbered you have not "made something". You made a mess is what you did. The only time I value sales like these is to dump old, stale inventory where getting your cash back is the consideration.

There is no such thing as a fair price. The only prices that matter are ones customers accept and ones that support your business. Hopefully, they are close. Yes, you will lose some business on price but that is OK. You do not want all the business—only the business you can turn profitably. Any other kind is practicing GOOB.

This being said, here are guidelines on pricing. For shop labor $70 an hour is about right. For "come to your place" labor is $95. Add $4.95 for MPS (miscellaneous parts, supplies, rags, oils) to all invoices and a fuel charge or mileage charge if the customer is outside the city. Most hard parts are priced at least double wholesale. Accountants get $150 an hour, lawyers $250. The bug man who comes to my house, sprays a little and leaves 30 minutes later, gets $85.

You will not be able to stay in business by trying to be the low price leader. Lowering prices by a small business owner just means you are now doing a bad thing that is designed for you to do more frequently. The lowest price game has already been won by big box retailers, mail order, and the internet. You have to charge more but you can justify it by being worth more. It goes on all the time or else Wal Mart would be the only company there is.

Never let salespeople set prices. **A salesperson never meets a price he thinks shouldn't be lower.** For this reason the OE must be very cautious giving credibility to a salesperson's suggestions on pricing. It does happen that salespeople just get beat by the competition who was better at doing his job. But I have never heard a salesperson say that the reason for the loss was that he just got beat, he just got outsold. I have never heard those words out of a salesperson's mouth.

Salespeople have a lot of pride and sensitive egos. These can do damage to the company and the rest of the sales department if, say, a rep gets too vocal about a deals he lost and blames it on his company's prices, a service technician, his manager, or anything else but himself.

Price-selling people frequently fall to The Greater Fool principle. Say you come upon a deal and a competitor is already in with a quote. The customer tells you what it is (which may not be true). It is low by your standards and you doubt the model quoted is right for this situation. What to do? Too often the answer is quote the same thing a little lower. So if the competitor is foolish in his price as well as recommendation, what are you? The Greater Fool. You should begin anew and have a better recommendation for the customer that will also bring better profit.

A big problem with discounting is that it is business cancer. Once discounting gets large or frequent salespeople doubt what a product is really worth. They lose confidence in it which lowers its profitability. Price selling is lazy selling. All professional sales people sell benefits, not price. Hold the line on amount of discount—10% maximum. Much higher discounting, combined with a scarcity of benefit selling, and you are GOOB and those selling like that are GOOBers.

Here is how you get the price you need: you actually earn it. How? By differentiating yourself from the competition. This means that your company: has better service, quicker response, more convenience, is easier to deal with, listens, provides needed advice, gives instruction, analyzes your real needs, picks up and delivers, provides a yearly rebate, has better selection, better hours, trains, has unique selection, has tenured employees, etc.

Provide this added value and the customer will provide you added pay. For example, NetFlix took down Blockbuster by adding the extra convenience of movies by mail and the value of no late charges. If a customer says a deal comes down to price he is really saying you have not distinguished yourself from your competitor in any meaningful way. Pricing is the only thing left for him to go on. The more your product has become 'commoditized' the more this is your dilemma. Lead with price, die with price. Once your product has hit commodity status (meaning me too!) it is time to look for some new and more profitable products to sell.

Your talents need to find added value for the customer. You will get paid a price you like. For example, everyone knows convenience stores charge more for everything but you pay because they add convenience. You can mail a letter for 42 cents and worry or pay FedEx $10 to get it there pronto and not worry. Fed Ex adds peace of mind and speed. So be the Fed Ex and convenience store of your industry.

It is important to raise prices yearly. I speak of the 5% -10% to neutralize inflation. You know that every year most of your costs go up because most suppliers increase prices to you. It is normal. Check for yourself. If you go three years without raising you are 15% in the hole on your bottom line because you neglected pricing. Your increases may irritate a few customers but most accept them. You cannot afford to eat increases to your business.

I must pause to quiz you so yes, this is a pop quiz. If you buy a product for $50 and sell it for $100, what is the markup as a per cent? What is the gross profit margin? 100% is the answer on the markup and 50% is the gross profit margin. **Mark up and gross margin are different things** but people get them confused. Here is another. If your target 50% gross margin on a product costing

$65, how do you find the selling price? Some take $65 x 150% for a $97 sale price. That formula produces 33% gross margin, *not the 50% you were looking for.* Take the wholesale price, $65, divide it by the inverse of the gross margin you are looking for, .50. This gives you the selling price that nets you 50% gross margin--$130 in this case. Understand this crucial difference or get a surprise visit from Mr. T.

People who pay for things rarely complain. It's the guy that you give something to that you can never please.
.....Will Rogers

Gross Profit is King

As you keep score as OE it is vital to count gross profit dollars not sales dollars. Business owners who brag about sales revenue and constantly count sales revenue are counting the wrong thing! This can get you in trouble. Gross profit is the money you keep after paying the manufacturer's cost for the products you sold or the labor costs you paid service people for the service revenue billed. That is the important money. It is the only money really yours. Brag about your gross profit. These are the dollars you are in business to get. They are the only dollars that really matter. Revenue just does not tell much. A car dealer may sell a $50,000 vehicle "at invoice" and make little. Real estate companies brag about "millions sold" but the true revenue to a real estate company is only its share of the 6% sales commission and not the sale price. If a sale has revenue of $10,000 and 20% GPM it brings the owner $2,000 to keep. If a sale brings $5,000 with a 40% GPM it brings the same $2000 on half the revenue. These two transactions have benefitted their company equally though one's revenue is double the other's.

There are huge companies with huge revenues that still fail. Large revenue is no guarantee of success. These companies did not generate enough gross profit on that revenue to succeed. Gross profit is king! It takes more business acumen to generate gross profit dollars than revenue dollars. Businesses do sell stuff and make few dollars on it. What's the point? Turning revenue for little or no gross profit begs the question of what you are doing and why are you doing it? It is nothing to brag about. Quite the opposite. In my sales department we do not even count sales revenue. The sales board and quotas are in gross profit dollar targets. **Gross profit is one of the truer indicators of how things are or aren't. Sales revenue is down the list.**

The law for staying in business is the same for everybody: over time, **gross profits** must be greater than expenses plus principle payments. This always works. If you say revenues are growing so we must be making money does not always work and you would be considered a knucklehead anyway. No mystery. Sometimes a little 'trickery' can buy you a few years. But in the long run, this law rules. Period. Count GP and avoid GOOB.

Back to pricing. People pay more if they like it more. Fact is, price is usually down the list as reasons people buy something. The number one reason they buy is they have the most trust or confidence in a product or company. That is why brand names do better than non-brand. Number two is they want it or need it or both and third is price.

As an exercise go around the room in a sales meeting and ask what people paid for homes. If $200,000 was an answer I showed there were $175,000 homes for sale in that neighborhood—a lot cheaper. Why not buy one of those? Usual answer: "We just did not *like* it as much." Same can be said for purchases of cars, clothing, running shoes, whatever. Work on making your business and products more *desirable, likeable.* Show happy people using them. Use color. Show unique ways they are used to maximize their value. Show how they provide unseen benefits. This is known as **marketing and is a source of additional gross profit margin.**

Selling the Right Stuff

Picking the right product is as important as getting pricing right. **The best product to sell to ensure long term success is one that creates additional revenue streams.** The razor sale that brings the lifetime of shaving cream revenue is a famous example. An Ipod sale brings a bazillion music downloads a year at 99 cents each. Now they are doing movies at $14 each. A copier sale brings service and supply stream revenue of toner and paper. A dairy cow throws off milk and cheese for its lifetime. Software generates support billing and upgrades. Cinema owners know when they sell a movie ticket they get a drink sale and probably popcorn. Both products have much higher gross profit percentages than the movie ticket. HP has made an absolute fortune not by selling laser printers but ink for them. They price ink near the price of gold, put little tabby things on cartridges so no one can duplicate them, and watch their ink business grow due to printer sales. These are products that "eat and drink." If one sold microwave ovens or mailboxes then the sale is the end of the relationship and the revenue stream. One and done products are GOOBish.

To illustrate the power of the eater/drinker product I relate how recently, a major company that has 30 of our water purifier units, called and said they needed filter changes. Each unit change is $165 and does, indeed, ensure pure water. But the point is that this amount of business, nearly $5,000 with decent profit, is *built in*. The cooler unit was simply in need of what it "eats and drinks" no matter what the economy is doing. No sales call was even necessary. What better than a product that creates its own demand?

To make the eaters and drinkers even a better sell yearly or longer service, supply and support contracts for them. Any type of contract business greatly reduces your risk of business failure. Contracts provide predictability and stability.

Another stable product segment are industries not obsoleted by technology advancements. Essentials for staying alive are good here such as food, water, medicine and shelter. I particularly like the water cooler product my company sells because the need for water will always be. You are on pretty safe ground if you operate any type of medical facility. A dairy? A chicken farm? An apple orchard? Heating and air conditioning? Manufacturing roofing materials? "Green" products?

Retailing is the riskiest business for the entrepreneur. The reason is that there is little compelling the customer to return, such as a contract. With the eaters and drinkers *they have to return*. For small retailers the long run rarely pans out. All it takes is for your area of town to go down or a big box retailer to appear and things can turn bleak in a hurry. Restaurants, bars, and little shops are among businesses with the highest mortality. Good for a while and then not. Success depends on good location and good locations have a way of becoming has been locations. Outbound businesses, ones that do not rely on a good location nor rely on the public coming in, remove this possible downfall from the equation.

The strategy a small retailer needs to minimize risk is to have an outside sales effort. Hiring salespeople, setting up an interactive website, advertising, putting on seminars are all good. Just waiting and hoping they come through your door is not. My hobby is woodworking and I like what my local shop does to pull in business and obtain residual business. It sells a six session course on various "how to" topics in woodworking. There is the session on "Producing Great Looking Finishes" and "How to Get the Most Out of Your Saw" and so on. These tutorials whet your appetite for more. They are held at convenient times in the evening and on Saturday's. The cost is $175. There are usually ten to fifteen attendees. After completing the courses I purchased $1400 worth of stuff and go back regularly to buy more stuff for more projects. But this little shop is just not waiting for people to come in the door. Good design!

Service and Supplies

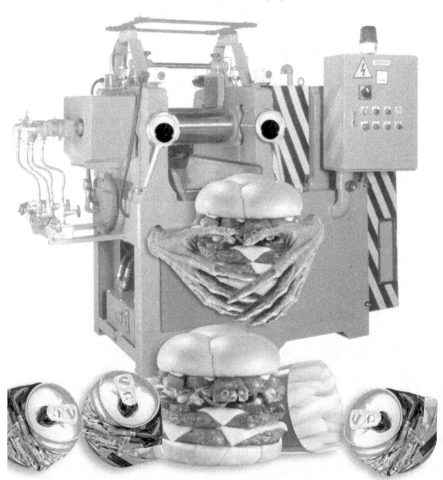

Eating and Drinking Machine

Do not sell a commodity-- a ubiquitous product that is bought at many places solely based on lowest price. Examples: gasoline, office supplies, computers, Levis, and maybe anything sold on the internet. Include these types in your offerings but not as the main course.

The success of your small business, its profitability, is going to come from *value added*. You add value by providing informed guidance on the right model a customer needs, having outbound service, providing training and instruction and repair services and showing ways to use something. Having convenient locations with long hours adds value. Indulging a little, I speculate the ultimate value added business might be making engines for the Space Shuttle. The least value added business? Maybe a self serve car wash.

If you sell a product heavily advertised by the manufacturer then the manufacturer is adding most of the value and gets the lion's share of the profits. A car dealer is an example. But if you are, say designing kitchens, you are adding most of the value and get gross profit margins three times higher than a car dealer.

Design Elements	
Prices Are Usually Set Too Low.	*There Is No Such Thing As A Fair Price.*
Raise Prices Annually.	*Figure Prices Correctly.*
Earn Your Price. Provide Value.	*Sell "Eaters and Drinkers."*

Positive Cash Flow
"I am positive I have no cash"

- A business owner

Lack of enough cash on hand, or at least due in any minute, is cited as small business' biggest headache. Small businesses are usually undercapitalized meaning their working capital is not what it needs to be. It is said the term "undercapitalized small business" is redundant. Small businesses graze on cash the same way cows do grass—all day every day. A small business can always, always use more cash. As OE, learn to look at the cash flow of everything you do. Take advantage of all loans as a source of cash. I say "all loans" because, as I write, and in the near future, things are so tight credit is not abundant. The credit standards have been mandatorily raised for everyone due to bailouts, TARPS, foreclosures and bankruptcies.

I remember my first encounter with the cash flow bogey man. In the early days Jerry handled the checkbook. I was selling up a storm and one day asked how much cash we had. "You mean right now? None." I was horrified but more of those days were ahead. It does not mean you are broke but it says you have a combination of problems such as poor cash flow and lack of working capital. Both need to be increased to keep bucks in the bank.

Ideal working capital is the sum of one month's expenses and debt service, one month's cost of goods sold plus AR. Not maintaining adequate working capital is stressful. It consumes needed business oxygen as your staff juggles who to pay when, how much, who is calling, etc. This sucks valuable neuron transmissions from the OE brain which inhibits good decision making which makes business ownership not fun. Let us prevent such and give this topic an important examination.

We begin with accounts receivable, better known as AR, one of the largest factors affecting positive cash flow.

AR is like people. It ages, turns delinquent, gets written off and goes to court. AR is parasitic to working capital. When you sell a customer on credit you get an IOU, not cash, even though you delivered all goods and services. It is the classic case of Wimpy saying he will gladly pay you Tuesday for a hamburger today. Then Tuesday turns into Friday and this decreases cash flow. This is the nature of a credit business. If you did not offer credit you will lose business. At year end you will have some bad debt—uncollectable AR. Hopefully not more than 5% of outstanding receivables. Whatever it is, it decreases cash flow and profit with it.

Once you have billed an invoice it lands on AR. This means you have also paid sales tax to the state on it (unless the customer is non-taxable). That is additional cash out until the invoice is paid. The sales tax in our state is high, nearly 10%. You might consider crediting older invoices, those in 60-90+, because you will get the sales tax back on them once they are deducted from the current month's revenue, thus increasing cash flow.

If you have a cash business then you do not have much AR. This is a good thing. Customers must pay before they leave with product. This leads to a business having prized products called 'cash cows" that continually turn great cash from high profit margins. I have never had a cash cow or even a calf. Examples might be women's cosmetics, Viagra, Harley Davidsons, lottery tickets and Starbucks coffee.

Listed below are other ways of increasing cash flow, other than robbing a bank, to increase cash flow.

> Since you cannot spend AR (but can borrow against it) you need someone working it to ensure it turns into real money. There are great payers and then those that take as long as you allow. This is just human nature or business nature as they, too, try to preserve cash at your expense. I have a saying: **everyone is trying to make their numbers at the expense of the other guys numbers."** It is harder to turn down a payment request on the phone as opposed to a letter in the mail. This is a serious and important job. Sometimes owners scrimp and just haphazardly make collection calls to save the expense of a full time person. This will cost you more than it saves. What good is it to improve your profit some but write off more in bad debt?

> Immediately spend less or delay spending. Very logical, harder to do. Anything you stop spending on increases cash flow. Getting terms extended can do this (force the extensions?). Buy used stuff instead of new.

> To improve cash flow change terms from net 30 to net 10. Maybe even to Net Now. Do not lean on anyone until 30 days. For customers in 90 days (accounts deceivable?) you may need a collection attorney. They get 30% of collected amount but are good at it. Better than nothing and they do the battling for you.

> Delay payables as much as vendors allow. This can vary quite a bit. Some are really on top of it and some are not. For the ones that are not take some advantage and don't

pay until they honk. You then appear as their AR issue which may psychologically make you feel better.

➤ Bill daily to increase cash flow. The sooner the bill goes out the sooner the money comes in. Some companies batch billing waiting until they have a little pile. Big mistake. If you wait two weeks to bill $10,000 then it is two weeks longer before the cash comes. Why would you do that? Some field/service reps have wireless hand held computers tied to the home office computers that cut invoices right after leaving the customer's office in order to increase cash flow.

➤ Limit inventory to increase cash flow—at least inventory you have to pay for within 30/ 60 days. You want to sell inventory by the time the bill is due otherwise it drains working capital. You will never get this one perfect but you try. With next day delivery available on most anything it is not necessary to stock a lot of stuff and this preserves working capital. There is no worse transaction in business than to buy inventory and it never sells.

➤ Work vendor terms as best you can and then pay the bill with a credit card. This improves cash flow by getting another 30 days to pay interest free. Plus you may earn frequent flyer miles. Our state recently took credit cards for sales tax payments giving 30 more days to pay which is a good thing on something this large.

➤ One of the best positive cash flow ideas is to get a customer to prepay for a product—or at least give you a deposit. This is a sort of reverse aging. Not too many will want to do this but you might offer some incentive for it like a small discount.

➤ Borrowing money is a source of positive cash flow. This can be from a bank of course. Try well-heeled others that you know well. Relatives too. The benefit for them is that the amount of interest you pay is double what they get elsewhere. Bank borrowing is very tight these days so other avenues need to be considered.

➤ Sell assets. Lease-back assets. Ebay is a worldwide market where people buy anything. A can of air, supposedly wind from Hurricane Katrina, sold for $10. Ebay does not bring the best price but it brings a price. Another way to sell assets is to a leasing company, who pays you cash for the asset, and then leases it back to you. This is like borrowing but lease companies look at things differently from a bank. Check the yellow pages for a lease company. Finally, just advertise something you have for sale via local media.

➤ Make a profit. When you make money beyond all expenses you have positive flow. Retaining it, as opposed to the owner taking it, builds working capital. Making a profit, above an appropriate owner's pay, is difficult. Part of the reason is poor planning. When OE's lay out yearly projections no doubt they engage in some DWI. To avoid being damaged from those fantasies, and to keep yourself in the reality zone, overestimate expenses by 5% and underestimate revenues by 5% and this will help keep you grounded.

➤ Barter. Can you pay a vendor with inventory sitting around? This saves cash. Ask your suppliers if they would accept your product or service instead of cash. For example offer free security alarm service in return for free copier service.

➤ Factoring. Factoring means selling AR to a company called the factor. It is not a loan. Say you have $50,000 in AR and need cash now. A factor will pay cash for the AR if no older than 60 days. The payment amount varies but normally it is 90 to 95% of the invoice totals. It can be helpful if no bank loan is possible. The payment from the factor is not based upon your creditworthiness but on your customers'. The factor company will hold back something in reserve until the invoice is paid by your customer. Once sold though, the factor company assumes all risk for payment or collection. The International Factoring Association, factoring.org, can help you further.

➤ Increase inventory turns. Try to sell your inventory and collect the money from selling it before it is time to pay for it. The higher your inventory turns the better your cash flow.

"We're Making Money But We Have No Money"

Measure cash flow every month. It is the lifeblood of your company. My favorite way is to take profit or loss for the month and subtract principle payments on any loans. I have always used this method and it works well. I figure my YTD position using this too, and in my mind, it is my true profit or loss position, not the profit or loss from the income statement alone. Banks lean this way too.

The term "cash is king" is used frequently. Because cash is real and stuff on paper is, well, stuff on paper. For example, a millionaire is one who has a net worth of a million dollars. It has nothing to do with how much cash he has which may be, say, less than $100,000. He can still be a millionaire if all his possessions are theoretically sold and total a million dollars after paying off debt. This may never happen. But he may look and act like a poor man because his cash position is poor. The definition of a millionaire ought to be a person with a million dollars in the bank. That would reduce the ranks of 'millionaires' greatly, including myself. Cash may not be king but it sure does spend better than paper tigers.

When I began in business Ed, my CPA, taught me an important lesson on positive cash flow. My income statement said we were making a little money. But then Ed said that when I added in principle payments on things like company vehicles and term loans, I had a negative. "Well, how can I be negative when my income statement shows positive Ed? I don't get it."

The income statement has interest in it *but nothing for a payment of principle* on a bank loan or car loan, so make sure you allow for it. If you have monthly principle payments of $5000 and make $3000 that month, you went backward $2000 in real money. That is negative cash flow of course. Too much of this and you are screaming "we are making money but we have no money!" If this pattern continues it can run you out of business even if you are "profitable."

The opposite can be true too. Your income statement can show a loss but your cash flow is positive---the result of a lot of depreciation or amortization (non-cash expenses) hitting your statement. Cash flow is really a better indicator of the health of a business than the P&L, and is more accurate about the immediate state of the business. Banks usually give more weight to it than the P&L.

There is a third financial statement that measures cash flow. It is called "Statement of Changes in Financial Position" that tracks changes to working capital. When YTD working capital position shows a decrease of 25% or greater it is time to take measures to replenish it.

A bank line of credit is a great loan to get from a bank to replenish working capital. These loans usually use your AR and inventory for collateral and require a monthly reporting of such to the bank. You can just pay the interest on it but banks want you paying it down when inventory is sold and then letting it increase when you buy more inventory. LOC loans renew annually and have a floating interest rate.

I have mentioned 'non-traditional' financing methods to improve cash flow such as lease backs, factoring, leasing, and inventory financing. Banks do some of these so it is worth asking but here are four companies that do too: Wells Fargo, General Electric, CIT, and American General. Only Wells Fargo is actually a bank. These companies have offices in most major cities. Their interest rates are typically a little higher than banks but not by much.

Design Elements

Shoot for 1.75 to 1 ratio.   *Invoice daily.*
Limit inventory. JIT delivery.   *Have dedicated AR person.*
Change terms to net 10.   *Borrow against AR.*
Sell assets. Barter. Factor.   *Understand profit vs. cash flow.*

Using Technology
This software is for you!

Good use of technology is good for just about everyone. It should mean customers get the service and information they need when they need it. Tech advancements can increase job satisfaction of users. Business profitability should improve since technology is cheaper than hiring additional employees. These attributes fit nicely in our quest for good business design.

The use of technology keys on three important missions: finding more customers, keeping the customers you have and increasing your value to the customer.

It is vital for your company to keep up with the tech or you will fall behind your competition. You remember the popular IBM Selectric. As good as it was can you imagine how far behind your document turnaround would be if you were still using one instead of a word processing program. Or still using snail mail only instead of email. Or using land lines and no cells. Those are obvious ones. There are still others that are proprietary for your industry.

Look at technology as something that serves you and not the other way around. Any tech product hoping to sell today knows that it must be easy to use. Any aversion you or employees have of technology needs to end. Not maximizing the productivity of technology to benefit your business is GOOB. Technology has the ability to leap your business forward quicker than about anything. Keep up with it.

If your business has bottlenecks or obstructions you need to assume there is a piece of tech to solve them because there is. The Apple App Store is a great example. There are several thousand downloadable software programs that run on an Iphone or Ipod. The range of "apps", which is short for applications, is mind boggling and amazing. For example, from the Iphone you can process credit card transactions, track FedEx/ UPS packages, locate things via GPS, pinpoint traffic cameras, tie in a chip in your NIKE running shoes to the Iphone for distance, elapsed time and number of strides in a run. You can buy an app that creates bar-coded shipping labels. There seems to be no limit which is how you should think in terms of what technology can do for you. There is an app for that! Now if they could just invent something that makes sales calls...... Here are some things to be doing right now.

- Check scanning. Surely you are not driving to the bank anymore. The bank will put a check scanner on your desk from which you electronically scan checks into your account. This saves wasted time and gas and gets your money in there right away. Think of the traffic congestion scanning relieves as well.

- PURL. Stands for Personalized URL. Developed in the past five years to work with direct mail. A unique site is set up for each direct mail campaign and the site address is printed on the mail piece. When the respondent hits the site it welcomes the person by name and records the email address as a lead. It provides other promotional info as well and asks respondents for more. Visit MindFireIncPurls.com. for information. The industry claims this method gets double and triple the number of responses of direct mail.

- MFP. Stands for multi-function printer. No need for a printer and a fax and a scanner and a copier and all their attendant supply and service contracts if you have this machine. One MFP does all of this if connected to your network. MFPs can copy in black and white or full color. MFPs save time, footprint, and money. Speeds range from 15 copies per minute to 70.

- Scanning to e-mail. This is done with a computer hooked to a scanner but is easiest from an MFP. Scanning to e-mail eliminates faxing. Documents are sent over the internet. This is particularly frugal when it eliminates long distance fax phone charges. Since scanning to email works off of paper originals and not electronic text it can replace expensive UPS/FedEx overnight letters.

- Electronic filing. The paperless office will never be. In fact there is more paper in use than ever. An office with "less paper" is readily attainable. Documents are scanned and indexed and go to the equivalent of an electronic manila folder. Think Ipod for documents. Paper documents are expensive. The square footage devoted to storing paper, sometimes whole rooms or buildings, can be reduced to nearly nothing with a USB flash drive or other media. File cabinets, mini storages, file folders all make paper handling hard and it is slow to find pages. Electronic filing searches files like the internet does. You can search from anywhere there is a computer instead of going to the file cabinet. You can scan old files as well. This is called "back filing". Also think about electronic back up storage of critical documents in case of a natural disaster.

This is especially important in a hurricane or earthquake prone area. Hurricane Katrina wiped out many businesses not because their building went down but because their business documents went down. Objective: No more manila file folders.

- E-mail invoices. Get the customer's OK and send invoices via email. This is immediate. There is no postage or paper. This makes a very low carbon footprint. Next, get the customers' permission to auto draft payment from their account for your invoices and you have it made! There is a website that can help you with this: zumbox.com.

- USB Flash drives, a.k.a. thumb drives and jump drives. The size of a half stick of gum, these devices plug into a USB drive in your laptop. They are amazing storage units that can hold 64GB of data--hundreds of thousands of pages. Think of them as file cabinet, DVD player, electronic brochure, all in your pocket. I have this book stored on one. Technicians can be issued drives with their tech manuals on them. While on a service call just plug it in and research the problem. These drives make it simple to carry data and easily transfer it to another computer. Flash drives are good for data back up. Have them made up with your company story or price list and give them to customers while on a sales call. Store pictures or videos on them. They are cheap, about $10 loaded with your data. A 32 GB flash drive sells for $130. I nominate these things for most usable piece of tech out there.

- Web Conferencing. Use web software, such as GoTo Meeting, that lets you have a conference with other offices or use it to make a sales call with companies in town or out. Saves travel expenses. When used for sales calls lets you use all your "guns and ammo" since you are broadcasting from your main office where your equipment is and can be demonstrated.

- Device Management Software. There is software to monitor all office machines, tell you how they are being used, how often, by who, if they are underutilized, over utilized, running out of memory or toner, need a service call etc. Most of them will actually email the servicing vendor that a call is needed without you doing anything. Same with emailing in their meter readings. It is not expensive. Get it and save many headaches. Have the data at hand to make an informed decision if a machine needs upgrading or replacing.

- Electronic Forms creation. If your business requires forms you may be having them preprinted. Of course, there are always changes that obsolete them and waste your preprints. This software lets you change forms and print them on demand from your MFP or laser printer. This saves waste and allows immediate updating of any form.

- Smart Boards. Great for any conference room where presentations take place. A large white "board" is actually a viewing screen that will operate the computer or internet by touching the command icons on it. Will also print to a printer or can email from it. Gives the impression your company is "high tech".

- VOIP. Stands for voice over IP meaning your phone calls go through the internet and are 'free'. No more charges for long distance. It is available now for cell phones but the sound quality is not good nor consistent yet. Look into Skype.

- Cloud computing. This means your files and software programs are moved from your hard drive PCs to a 'cloud' you connect to via internet. This keeps from buying new hardware and software because the 'cloud' hosts it for you. Everything from spreadsheets to file storage goes to your cloud. Google is becoming the main cloud entry point. Gmail is in a cloud. Cloud computing is projected to be a 11 billion dollar a year business this year. Try Amazon's Elastic Compute Cloud. Cloud computing is a green solution. Electric use is much lower as is the hardware requirement. For Iphoners, check out Box.net which lets you access and store up to 1GB of files from your phone.

- To ID those blocked calls get trapcall.com installed. It tells you the phone number behind virtually any caller.

- Cell phones. Obviously. If they are issued by your company for business use do not sign for long distance capability, texting and all the rest. These things double the bill and are usually not necessary for local business use. You can get a cell phone for business use for a flat $40 per month.

These are technologies I am familiar with. Most are inexpensive and can pay for themselves. OE's need things like these to make their business and themselves more efficient, responsive, systematic and less dependent on employees. This increases profitability and holds down future cost increases. Be careful not to disappear into tech world though. For all the new advancements in communication people talk to each other less. There is endless email, texting, video conferencing and voice mail, all great tech, but these have made us less personal. It does not seem to have taken the stress out of the system either but put more into it. It has reduced the expectation response window to *right now.* Can anyone remember when you sent something air mail if you wanted it there really quick?

The business that can use the tech but increase its personal touch has the winning combination. Maybe if we all agree to turn off the 'press one for this and two for that' we

> *"Business success at the expense of family, marriage, health or faith is really failure."*

can start a revolution. Auto attendant answering, and the like, are not bad if you do not need a person. If you get familiar with the way a company works, the tech can ease you through what you need quicker than a person. The problem is that when you need a person quickly there is not one. The best answer is for customers to have the choice to follow an automated attendant or a real person, both promptly. This is what we do at my company.

SUMMARY OF
TOP REASONS BUSINESSES FAIL

- ➤ **Owner ignorance.** Owner does not get regular, vital information about the business and adjust accordingly. Does not know benchmarks for the business. Has poor controls.

- ➤ **Selling wrong product.** Product does not 'eat and drink'—produce additional revenue streams that are under contract.

- ➤ **Pricing inadequate.** Needs to be based upon burden rate and adjusted yearly. Eliminate free things.

- ➤ **Passion lost.** The drive and enthusiasm for the business have played out. Needed horsepower to make things go now not enough. Creative element gone.

- ➤ **Bad leadership.** Standards not set and checked. Communication inconsistent. Reclusive. Do not 'know' employees.

- ➤ **DWI.** Important decisions are ego based.

- ➤ **Financial focus is on revenue and not gross profit.** Revenue does not tell that much. Tracking gross profit is the telltale figure

- ➤ **Owner's time misused.** Owner not spending enough time on 'A' tasks. 'B' and 'C' tasks should be delegated. Learn your ABCs.

- ➤ **Law of Negativity.** Business and morale succumb to terminal negativity.

- ➤ **Partners.** Partnerships are based more on need than want. Eventually a problem.

- ➤ **Change monster.** You have been visited by Businessauress Rex and it got the best of things. Change is certain.

- ➤ **Business does not line up with personality.** You are independent but the business ties you down. You are creative but the business deals in detail. Mismatched.

- ➤ **No stress management.** Work all the time. No hobbies. No exercise. Business is an addiction. You and family burn down.

- ➤ **Not keeping up with technology.** A missed opportunity for your business to profit. It also causes you to lag behind in understanding how your customers work.

- ➤ **The Great Recession.** Enough said!

PART THREE:
Final Designs

Y ou have learned your lessons well and manned your post for years with courage, smarts and results. You have burned through your share of rocket fuel and now want to do something else. Welcome to Advanced Designs! I know how you feel since I have just been through this. It is maybe a more difficult stage than starting the darn thing.

Americans look upon small business ownership as one of the American Dreams. We know it does not always turn out that way. But it has for you. You are, in accomplishing this, part of the very success fabric that this capitalistic country represents. Congratulations.

This is a short section but it contains a great summary of all the best lines in the book as well as the *Top Eighteen Thoughts You Must Have To Stay In Business* to make sure you benefit from reading this book.

Advanced Design
I desire to retire

Your roaring 20's and 30's may start to turn into the boring 40's and 50's. This is especially so if you are of the true entrepreneurial profile and have run your course of ideas and creations. If not, that is good. But you may now have a successful, level business that offers you only the managerial role. However, you don't want it! These Middle Ages are dangerous in an OE's business life and personal life. Things are different and with this new dangers but opportunities too.

You may want to retire or begin to see that is your course. Certainly you do not shut down your creativities but pursue new ones not heavily invested in "profit and loss." What you are looking for in the Middle Ages is "profit and profit."

It only makes sense that as we age our wants change. Having spent 20 years in the ownership/managerial role may be enough for a lot of OE's. The mid-life years, indeed, bring crisis which has been documented in best-selling books such as *Passages*. Keeping in mind that one OE year is like one and a half 'normal' years. This means you worked 20 years but have really been doing it 30 some years! Enough!

The biggest danger of the Middle Ages is passion for the business is less. Maybe a lot less. Not to say it is not as important to you as ever or even more so, just that the rocket fuel has been burned. This is not a plus and is not good for your business either. It is important to recognize this and make adjustments accordingly.

There is damage to people and lives in mid-life. Marriages fail, health gets threatened, jobs lost, children leave home. Whatever you have been doing it has been for some time. Naturally you ask "is there anything else?" All this is even more critical for a business owner because so many others are involved. You do not want any of this to hurt your company or employees because it can. This chapter is about deciding to transition somehow to something else.

Moving to your next life level is easier to decide than to do. It is an evolved process planned for years. It is either that or sell the business if it can bring the retirement funds needed. We look at both.

Transitioning

While you have been proud to lead the charge of your company you can be just as proud to "work yourself out of a job" bringing others to roles you brandished. That is a sign of great success. Your goal is to go to the mailbox, get your paycheck each month and take it to the bank. You could electronic deposit but now have time and need to get out more.

But this is no easy row to hoe. There is no one like you and you really cannot be replaced. You are not going to be either. You are still going to keep an eagle eye on the financials and the performance of your people. You will go in each week for a time.

What is needed here is a strong, systemized company that knows what needs to be done most of the time without you.

The fun for you and the employees is handing them tasks and decisions you did. They may even do a better job than you if you birth new passion in them. Give them parameters for good decisions and let them make some. This is a morale booster and you should get satisfaction from it. Hand off duties in a planned manner and it should get you where you want to go providing you have people with potential. **I suggest, though, that you may be doing something even more vital than all that by doing this and that is *keeping yourself from losing the business.***

I could feel the changes. I began to leave work early since I was bored. I went to the gym which was a good use of time, and then home. Next I took off Wednesdays and Fridays. Then I just did not feel like going at all. I holed up in the den on the couch and didn't shave for a week. Didn't work out either. Certainly I was depressed but how could I be? I had a great wife and family, house, income, toys, blah, blah, blah. But no rocket fuel.

My VP, came to my house. "What's wrong Tom. You are not you. When are you coming to work? You have 30 employees there." "I know. I know. I just don't know how much longer I can keep doing this." Cindy was aghast. "It just does not motivate me anymore. I used to feel like a Jedi Knight and now it is R2D2. I fix problems, say yes or no, sign things but it is robotic."

I remember discussing this with Ed, my lifelong CPA. I said "Ed, I think I am burnt out." He said "No, you are not because you still want to get into something. You just don't know what." Which was a good piece of advice and turned out to be true. The company was fine, fighting all the usual battles but always ending the year with some profit. Four years earlier I was Memphis Small Business Executive of the Year. I was 48 years old. So now what? How did I get in this place"? I would ask myself.

Rocket Fuel Required

The company ran well without me. I had long term people who knew what to do. But it was me in danger, not the company. Deep down I knew if I did not figure this out it would affect the company and "my people" which made me feel distinct sadness. " Why could I no longer charge in there feeling confident, well dressed, successful, happy, energized? Heck if I knew. But I couldn't.

People sell companies at this point and that might have been an answer. Take some money and do something different. I could get several million dollars. Then all those trusting faces came into view and I knew I would never do that one since it would change their lives. They put their trust in me. Their well being is still the most important mission to me. All noble thoughts, yes, but they made me even more depressed! Man, where is the feel good?

My Dad said never make decisions under duress. So I resigned myself to taking my time, not doing anything rash, watching Oprah if necessary, and finding answers. You do not get much sympathy from friends. My best friend Gary, who I have known since IBM days, and I would have cigar night where he would hear me out: "Son, we are on search for your problems. People have real problems, like me keeping a job in this economy. And my ex-wife. Alimony. Now those are real problems." Every owner would do well to have a Gary in his corner to keep him grounded and ego/competitiveness out of the relationship which is, of course, difficult for men to do. I can always count on Gary for this. Gary can drive a golf ball farther than anyone but I can drive a car faster than he or anyone else can though.

What I needed, and did not realize, was a new TENE. You will recall this stands for Temporary Entrepreneurial Neuron Explosion. In other words, something that would generate new passion that secretes rocket fuel which I could then tank up on and burn.

So luckily one day I came across my ex-VP who left the company years earlier. I tried to talk her into coming back. She said the next thing she wanted was her own business. I told her I was in mid-life crisis mode and looking for something new as well. We were motorcycle enthusiasts so we conspired to open a Kawasaki dealership. We applied to the SBA for a building loan with working capital and got 1.3 million dollars. Wow. I was beginning to produce rocket fuel again.

The building went up and it was hard to believe. Then I was horror stricken wondering if people would come in the door. They did. Della and I both worked the sales floor for three years taking credit applications and all. We were on a mission not to fail and we didn't. We worked our way into the top 10% of Kawasaki dealers nationwide. It was just way too cool.

It did it for me. I got up every day and rode a motorcycle to work. I felt fine again. I said to my wife "well, it looks like starting Kawasaki was just the thing, huh?" Well, it ought to have. We had to borrow a million and half dollars to do it." Good point, my dear.

Then one day I told Della I just could not do this floor work anymore. It is just not me (translation: mission over). So I pulled back but she stayed on the floor. I slowly let go of a lot of and Della was happy to handle day to day. I still had my CFO from e/Doc Systems producing statements so I was in the loop.

Things are now clear to me and I know myself better. I left IBM for the same reason I "left" Corporate Copy for the same reason I left Kawasaki: burn rocket fuel or die. Speaking of rockets maybe that is what entrepreneurs are all about—putting themselves into orbit. They just do not want to return to Earth I suppose.

I can look back and know with certainty what I am— Entrepreneur. Entrepreneurs are about the trip and not the destination. About designing it, not operating it. Always about the mission and not the landing. The thrill of being important in people's lives. Seeing things where others don't. We feel everything intensely. We risk what others will not, possessing self confidence above all reason. Normal people may live on meat only or vegetables only but entrepreneurs require Soul Food.

Back to the important point of saving your business by handing it over. The more you are becoming a moody, uninspired loose cannon walking hallways the more you hurt the well being of your place and family too. Employees key on the mood and method of the boss and don't miss much, so you are not hiding anything. Honesty and reality are important here. My point is adjust best you can. Feed yourself new things, big or little, to keep painting that canvas. Turn over all you can then keep the rest. Maybe that will do it. Don't "risk it all", though, at the expense of the employees. This is your crises, not theirs. OK Jedi?

I am 59 and semi-retired from e/Doc Systems for the past five years. My son is there as well as my old hands to see to day to day. I bought a farm of 70 acres complete with tractor and bulldozer. Now I burn diesel fuel instead of rocket fuel. I am always dirty. Instead of Brooks Brothers I wear Carhartt. I really love it. I bond with my donkey, Dusty, and my two dogs, Pete and Sam. They constitute my 'posse'. I can't say that I seek the entrepreneurial bug anymore but then here I am writing this book that is actually going to publish. But it could happen. I saw an ad for a sawmill that was for sale near me and pulled it out of the magazine and said hmmmmm…

Selling It

Selling your business can be a thrilling day if it brings enough to retire and if you have other things you want to do. Barring that, I don't think you should do it or you will have the same problems you faced before selling it such as boredom and a feeling of no mission. If the future looks more challenging than you care for that can be a good reason to sell. I think the key thing is that you have something else that you have become passionate about. We know it needs to burn some rocket fuel. Even if you did not get "retirement money" you may get enough to turn your new passion into something that makes enough to make up the retirement shortfall. I have opened up the writing and farming lobes of my brain. I still oversee all 'A' tasks at e/Doc Systems however.

Formula For What It Is Worth

Selling a business brings heated talk about it's worth. There are books written on this and even people to hire to assess its value. Usually, owners think their business is worth more than it is, the same way people do with homes. In any case, I can give you the formula that will be close and no need to spend any money. Here it is: 3.5 times recasted cash flow. When you recast cash flow you calculate it by removing from your annual income statement all pay and benefits that have gone to you, plus interest, taxes, depreciation and amortization otherwise known as EBITDA. Also remove all occupancy expense if the business is being moved into the buyer's facility. Take that figure, add to it any annual profit you are showing, and this is the number you multiply by 3.5. A very high sale price would be five times this number. As a rough rule this works out to be a sale price of a little over half annual revenues for many businesses. Businesses are worth the most when annual inflation rate is low and they are worth less when inflation is running high.

Selling your business amounts to getting about five years total pay and benefits. The thing is, what will you do if this runs out? Best to take the proceeds and pay off everything so you can live on a lot less without worrying. The most profitable thing to do to get the most out of your business by retirement time is to keep it, if it has a stable future. You have delegated well and have good people so it is taking care of itself and you after all the years of it being the other way. If it can continue like this for the next decade, while still paying you, that is the biggest payoff of all.

Then there is this to consider: the Change Monster. We know that 70% of small businesses do not survive past seven years. This is a large number that means there are powerful dynamics in play that can force even well run businesses out for reasons they are not responsible for. It could be that, if your business is doing well right now, it is the perfect time to sell and thus "play the percentages" meaning you get the most for it while the getting is good and eliminate ever worrying if it will last the long run. Tough call, but it needs to be considered. You should especially consider it if your business is made up of just a few large customers. You have a greater chance of going from hero to zero than does a business with many customers each making smaller purchases but providing a steady base.

You will always get less money when selling a business if you are the business. Simply put, since you are the business and are not going with it, it stands to reason it has less value without you. These are typically businesses where the owner does everything from sell to pay bills and shares some of that with his spouse. If you plan to sell the business in the future you need to begin making it work more without you. That will help increase its value.

You will get more for a business if it can be folded into the buyer's facility. This eliminates duplicate expenses such as rent, the receptionist, office manager, two phone systems, two computer systems, two utility bills and so on. So if you are selling, time your lease expiration to coincide with your sell date.

Methodology of Selling the Business

There are two ways that a business is sold: stock sale or asset sale. Stock sales for small businesses are rare and not advantageous. They are more common for stock exchange companies or if a stock exchange company is buying yours which is rare too. So we will focus on the asset sale.

In an asset sale the buyer is buying the hard assets, the goodwill, customer lists and non-compete agreement from the owner. Those are the four main price points in an asset sale. The buyer does not buy any stock. This way, the buyer is assured he is not assuming any previous liabilities of the seller.

On the effective date of the sale all AR and AP, as of that date, remain with the seller. It should turn out that your outstanding accounts payable will be paid by the outstanding accounts receivable as it comes in. Any larger bank loans of the seller will have to be paid off from his purchase money. It may be that the buyer would agree to assume a loan but the lender would have to approve that plus this would lower your purchase price by the amount of the loan.

The seller will have tax to pay on the net gain from the sale price. However, this gain is shielded by the four elements I listed above which are tax deductible over a period of time. The sales will fall under the capital gains tax laws which means there is a tax rate of 15% on the gain. This is a much more favorable rate than having the gain fall under ordinary income.

The buyer may want a 'holdback' of 10% but the seller should not give it. The buyer wants as much assurance as possible, of course. The way to get that is to do a great job during the due diligence phase when the checking and inspecting of everything goes on. The other problem with holdback, which is usually kept for one year, is that the buyer finds reasons why he thinks he should keep it and from then on it is a hard legal deal that costs as much as the 10% maybe.

Speaking of legal again, if you are the buyer you want to specify that all legal costs be paid out of the seller's proceeds since he is the one walking away with the cash.

It is hard to sell a business without providing some owner financing. If you can get an all cash sale you are quite lucky. But taking back a note means you still have to worry with the business's well being so you have to judge if that is worth it. Make sure you have an ironclad credit worthy buyer. If there is non-payment you can get the business back and keep what you have been paid.

It takes a long time to buy or sell a business. If two people agreed today it might take six months to close. There is due diligence to be done which is auditing books, tax returns, inventory and any pending litigation. If a bank loan is involved it needs time. If lawyers are involved there may never be enough time. Kidding. You usually should have a lawyer but they can hijack the proceedings over tangential issues that they consider important but you do not.

Duress Sale

As the 70% business failure rate shows, many businesses get into trouble they just cannot solve or cannot get things profitable. Yet, they may have something to sell to a similar competitor who can absorb the seller's customers and contracts and for whom this is added business. It is worth something and worth buying.

Selling what you still have while you still have it is better than going down until there is nothing left. If you are in a duress situation use the same business evaluation formula I have given and approach your competitors with it. You will not be in a real strong situation but you may find several competitors are interested. They provide a mini bidding war that might help the price increase.

You will certainly like to get cash for what you are selling but let's say the buyer is not willing to get a bank loan or cannot. You can still sell it between the two of you with owner financing. Get a lawyer to draw up documents that protect you if the buyer defaults in any way. Another good possibility in all this is that you may be able to be hired by the bigger competitor for at least a period of time. That is not only an income situation for you but it helps you see that the purchase goes well. It could even be that the whole 'purchase price' is put into a larger than normal salary for you under an Employment Contract for say three to five years.

Designs for Crazy Times

Anyone writing anything in 2009 stands a good chance of being wrong or being broke or maybe both. Certainly these are unprecedented financial times. If we look though, we can see some things that tell us if there is light at the end of the tunnel or an oncoming train.

One certainty is this is a great time to buy anything. Prices will never be lower. The same is true for interest rates if you can get a bank to part with their (our?) cash. Just about any hard good sold is on sale at prices never to be seen again. The same is true for real estate. Prices have dropped about twenty per cent across the board. There is a question mark there, though, if it will appreciate as it once did. Probably. But it will take about five years to recover that 20% lost. The reason prices should recover are many. The population continues to grow so it will need more places to live. Housing starts have plummeted so, as inventory is sold, it is not being replaced which will drive demand. When this happens is anyone's guess. And, of course, they are not making land anymore.

Here are other guesses:

> There have been a great many business failures. The majority have been in the retail area or B2C-business to consumer. B2B-business to business has done a lot better. Staying out of the retail sector would seem wise.

> The government is printing trillions of dollars to be put into the economy to get it going again. If it does then the after affect of the government issuing so much money is inflation—the rising of all prices. This will be good for home values, bad for mall customers. It will be wise to plan for inflation ahead.

> With layoffs in the US at a record level, double the normal amount, it would seem there would be a lasting effect on

employees' minds. They may value their jobs more than ever. Employers could feel they have the upper hand and become more demanding. More will try and open their own businesses. It has even been suggested that in the future job openings will go to the lowest bidder.

➢ Things are going to change! No matter what is going on now, you know that change is going to be the case later! This one is always true. I'm starting to like the..well next year it will be just the opposite... theory. It seems to usually be the case.

➢ There are many businesses under duress right now so it could be a good time to purchase a competitor or a company with a similar mission to yours. You might get a call asking if you wanted to sell your business.

➢ If gas is going to spike higher in the future it will devalue homes and businesses at the most distance from work or shopping concentrations.

➢ Slicker communication devices/software will be in demand to cut the expense of travel. Commercial real estate may suffer as business owners see it as one of their highest expenses. Telecommuting, teleconferencing and who knows what future technology will have us all working faster than ever without even meeting each other or going into a building. Dataquest says that 28% of the workforce now works from home. Do we really want to eat, sleep, play, bathe and work in the same small structure 24/7? Would it be mentally healthy?

➢ Products are going to de-content. There will be fewer in the box or bag—although the container may get even bigger! The product will weigh less. You will have to pay for features that were once included. This will be a method to increase profitability while manufacturers strive to create the image that everything has stayed the same. Whether you should use this approach or a version of it is something to study.

> "Green" businesses are a good bet. Energy costs will do nothing but increase. Energy users will always be open to how to spend less on energy and help the environment. Any feature that makes your product greener can is a boasting point. Make yourself a student of green. It is high profile.

> Businesses that cater to do-it-yourselfers look good. The economy has doubled the usual unemployment rate and that means many are looking for ways to cut costs. Doing their own car repair, home repair, looking for used anything, should be a trend that may last.

> Americans have quit spending on anything other than necessities. They have put credit cards in a holster. Well, on the positive side it means pent up demand to be released sometime. Whoever can judge that one right should do well. The consumer is understandably reigning in but that causes the recession to be worse. Those with a stable situation could help by not postponing major purchases. Although nobody would blame you if you did.

I have mentioned that Federal Express world HQ is here in Memphis as is its considerable brain trust. The head of Federal Express IT, Rob Carter, was quoted in *Time* magazine saying he thought the best training for anyone who wants to succeed in the future workplace is the online game *World of Warcraft*. *Time* says there are 10 million users worldwide playing the game.

Players face obstacles to be overcome, called Quests. The one contributing the most gets to lead his team until someone else contributes more. To solve the Quests takes intense collaboration, is constantly demanding and surprising. Said Carter: "It takes exactly the same skill set people will need more of in the future to collaborate on work projects. The kids are already doing it."

Staying in Business by Good Design!
Putting it all together for best design

Our last chapter is concentrated info gathered from the highlighted lines from previous chapters into one final chapter. It lines out the best practices and avoids the things that lead to going out of business. Just tear out this last chapter and carry it as a cheat sheet.

1) We know that a big reason for the 70% failure rate of small businesses is that the owner just was not right for small business ownership. To avoid this we:

> *Stick with what we know. Have some experience.*

> *Try some commissioned sales work first.*

> *Understand our predominant traits and harmonize with them.*

> *Know that keeping it going is harder than getting it going.*

> *Must recruit well to get the help to be successful.*

➤ *Register a "10" on the passion, motivation, knowledge categories.*

2.) Trouble is going to be our constant companion. The majority of things in a day are not positive. We accept this and:

➤ *Stay physically and mentally fit.*

➤ *Invoke The Eye of the Tiger. We concentrate, stay determined, positive.*

➤ *Reduce overall pay instead of laying anyone off.*

➤ *Get every employee into cost cutting mode.*

➤ *Increase revenue by raising prices, add ons, and selling new products.*

➤ *Don't buy the building.*

➤ *Know there is always something that can be done. There is.*

➤ *Play hardball. You are loud, persistent and demanding. Lawyer backup.*

➤ *Hire a consultant on a month to month fee basis only.*

➤ *Identify any trouble OE is causing in particular.*

3.) You are the leader so everyone must know what you stand represent. You will do this through repetition, using Confucius communication principle, and being a great communicator. But you will also:

➤ *Always inject positive juoo juoo into the business atmosphere.*

➤ *Have fun as Chief Morale Officer.*

➤ *Treat everyone differently! Work with everyone as an individual.*

➤ *Become the Employee Godfather.*

➤ *Not try to give what you do not have.*

> ➢ *Think of it as you work for the employees not the other way around.*

> ➢ *Keep ego out of it!! Expensive otherwise!!*

> ➢ *Measure everything you need to manage.*

4.) Price points and product selection are crucial to your success. Most OE's set prices too low so you may need an increase. Best products to sell are ones that bring in additional revenue streams.

> ➢ *There is no such thing as a fair price.*

> ➢ *Raise prices annually. Figure them correctly.*

> ➢ *Fix prices based upon burden rate.*

> ➢ *Earn your price. Provide value and differentiation.*

> ➢ *Revenue does not tell you much but gross profit does.*

> ➢ *Sell "eaters" and "drinkers".*

5.) Salespeople are among the most, if not the most, valuable people in the company. Nothing happens until somebody sells something.

> ➢ *Above most in enthusiasm. Must be continually fed.*

> ➢ *Difficult to manage.*

> ➢ *Salespeople not in control half the time, customer is.*

> ➢ *"Athletes" of the business world.*

> ➢ *Toughest job in business.*

> ➢ *Reps reach best potential if don't job hop.*

> ➢ *Need help with detail.*

> ➢ *Need enforcement of their time management.*

> ➢ *Need to use CRM software.*

6.) The owner must know a lot of things and have an actual "A" game. Lack of knowledge is major business failure element.

> ➢ *Trends of financial ratios is most informative thing.*

- *Legal--depends if you are plaintiff or defendant. Always expensive, slow.*
- *Things are going to change. Beware the CHANGE MONSTER!*
- *Know where to spend your time. Rate tasks A,B,C.*
- *OE needs to work on 'A's and delegate the rest.*
- *"P" laws.*
- *Learn your benchmarks. Will lead you to profitability.*

7.) Cash flow issues are small business' number one money problem. Everyone is trying to make their numbers at the expense of the other guy's numbers.

- *Know how to figure your working capital. Shoot for 1.75 to 1.*
- *Limit inventory. Try to attain 'just in time' delivery.*
- *Keep eagle on on AR. Get attorney for over 90.*
- *Keep payment terms short to net 10 or due upon receipt.*
- *Invoice daily. Delay payables.*
- *Sell assets, barter, and factor to get more flow.*

8.) OE must be tech savvy. Technology is "more productive" than people. Makes significant difference in profitability.

- *Paperless office not possible but 'less paper' office is.*
- *Use tech to cut down drive time and response time to customers.*
- *Flash drives amazing storage device, back up device, promotion device.*
- *MFP is one device in four—printer, scanner, copier, fax, color copier.*

9.) You are your biggest and toughest competitor. There is more profit to be found tightening your ops and overcoming your resistance zones.

> *Be the Designer in Chief. Design for the bigger money.*

> *Improve your ability to compete.*

> *Know differences in B2B marketing and B2C marketing.*

> *Launch new things continuously.*

> *Swoop don't scoop.*

> *OE must produce unique creations.*

> *Overcome your resistance zones.*

10) Mid-life meets the CHANGE MONSTER. Design heads for the end zone.

> *Turn over responsibilities or sell?*

> *Continue to guide.*

> *Business will sell for close to 3.5 times recasted cash flow.*

> *Either way, you will need to have new things you want to do.*

> *Designs for crazy times.*

We have continuously talked about the 70% failure rate after seven years but there is a 30% success rate as well! Not only that, but the 70% failure rate does not take into account such things as whether the OE was simply able to close the business, or sell it to someone, without any loss or serious loss. So our success number is at least somewhat higher.

Many of the bad design elements are not hard to overcome if they can be recognized as such. This recognition is a major moment to the continuation of your enterprise. Not being a know-it-all, listening and continuing to learn, are signs of someone whose brain can still be fertilized and grow.

The number one element of initial success, as well as continuing success, is inspired *passion* coming out of the owner. It is a powerful force, is rocket fuel, and is the magic ingredient that is going to overcome all adversity if it is to be overcome. OE's, and those supporting him, need to guard this priceless propellant like Fort Knox guards gold. After all, how far would the best designed rocket travel without rocket fuel? Same for the entrepreneur/owner.

I believe the number one factor that takes down a business is the CHANGE MONSTER. It is a broad category. Powerful, cannot always be foreseen, and not always in one's power to stop it if seen. This should keep you humble even amidst jubilant success. Just knowing things are always going to change is a good defense against it. It can take down the biggest of companies who have even million dollar salaried minds on staff. It can even be that you are running your small company better than say, General Motors, Circuit City Blockbuster or Bank of America.

Your best weapon for continued success, along with yourself, is your Band of Brothers and Sisters who stand with you. They are your Special Forces, each uniquely important to you and your company. Treat them like family. Make company resources available to help them solve problems. Treat them as individuals. Treat them all differently. If you are one who cannot bond with people then best you stay very small as a company.

To keep your company relevant through the years keep adding value to it by increasing what it can do for your customers. If their needs change you have to change. Sell the eating and drinking products and get customers under contract. Stay away from operating small retail shops or businesses that depend on selling a famous brand. You are not adding much value to that equation and are the most vulnerable to change. The manufacturer will have a lot of clout here. Whatever you do, have an outbound sales effort and do not depend on sufficient 'inbounders' walking through your front door. Risky, risky.

Keeping your prices current will help keep you in business as will adding more products that provide additional revenue after their sale. Remove the word 'free' from your vocabulary. Charge for everything but, at the same time, deliver more value to your customers than your competitors do. Getting customers under contract provides protection for your business from sudden change and gives a longer lead time if they are going to cancel. Do not be afraid to ask for a contract longer than a year. Remember to track gross profit revenue more than anything else and that revenue is a lesser indicator of how things are. Think in terms of gross profit and not revenue.

Speaking of revenue, though, we do love positive cash flow! Cash coming in is always a good thing. It does happen that sometimes the goals of profitability and life sustaining prices have to be put secondary to turning creaky inventory into cash to keep up working capital. But we cannot live on a steady diet of that. Working capital is to a business what blood is to a human—necessary to continue! It is the blood bank. Work hard to get your ratio to 1.75 to 1. Having AR worked constantly and keeping inventory low will help keep cash in the checkbook. Being profitable also helps. You will have to borrow from time to time too.

To be a champion OE you are going to have to be physically fit. I say this more for the benefit of your mind than the body itself. The mind follows the body and vice versa. You have control of that equation by keeping up the body with regular exercise. I am sure you keep up the vehicles, computers and such that help you do business. You are more important than that so break out the NIKEs! It will improve your business IQ and help tank up the rocket fuel.

Maybe there is no greater mistake an OE makes than putting his time in the wrong places. Remember our 'A' task principle. If you want to get an "A" in entrepreneurship spend most of your time on 'A' tasks. Tackle the big problems most of the time and with your best stuff. Delegate the B and C. You want to spend your time on designing for the big money. Remember, you are the Designer In Chief. Ideally, as the years go by you should be working yourself out of a job if you are doing it right.

If I am an employee of yours I want to know that you know something. You expect me to know how to balance my ledgers, repair machines or sell. I want to know that you, as my employer, are as firmly in control of the facts of your situation as you want me to be in mine. I count on this as does my family. Employees will want to see you demonstrate your prowess now and then by solving crises, hiring skilled workers and seeing your efforts bring in business. Can you execute? Are you executive material?

Make one of your 'A' tasks *designing for sustainability*. That is really the theme of this book. Forget breaking sales records, being number one, getting big, looking good, beating the other guy. These could be helpful but they are also full of dangers. None of these are the least bit impressive if you are no longer in existence. Some of these companies are merely doing a bad thing in a bigger way. Let designing for sustainability occupy a top rung among your business motivators. You want to be the diesel powered long haul trucker and not the quick stop/start sports sedan.

Lets never forget the OE himself is big competition. The success of your business is in direct relation to, and limited by, what you know how to do and how well you execute. You need to know your financials, your legal, your ratios, benchmarks, your laws and principles but knowing yourself may be the hardest of them all. Learn the areas where you resist action or lack expertise and those would be your work zones. You are competing against those. And please, please, keep your ego out of as much decision making as you can. It is business DWI—Deciding While Intoxicated. Hopefully someone will issue you a citation before you hurt people.

As you compete against yourself, and others, you will be limited by the amount of energy that comes off of you and out of you. Stay fit, mentally and physically, so that you may launch continuously and abide by the Law of the Pinball. Also, keep something in reserve to do battle with the Change Monster when it decides to visit. Spend that business IQ of yours on 'A' tasks.

Technology today is a wonderful thing and a true servant. Search for what you need it to do and you will probably find it. Use those little flash drives. Work on using less paper because paper slows down offices. The tech needs to make you closer to your customer, not farther away. It is there to make your business more responsive.

Congratulations if you are where you can smell the end zone. That calls for its own design. It takes a few years to get it in place but eventually you need to hand the business over to younger folks burning rocket fuel or sell it so you can retire. You can keep at it, sure. You may have to. But you are not going to do it as well as you once did. This will not be the best thing for something as demanding as small business ownership. Remember my analogy that business owners and salespeople are like athletes and even the greatest of those peak and decline.

Letting go either way is not a very good idea if you do not have other things that consume other passion you hopefully have to take the place of the business. As we get older we should skew it all more in the direction of spending more of our time on just what we like to do and try to leave the rest. It is not about profit and loss anymore, but profit and profit!

The Top Eighteen Thoughts

To close out I am going to follow what seems many readers like and that is a Top Ten List or the X Amount of Good Habits you should have. I will take everything this book has said and reduce it to eighteen short print bites. I am not stating that I have done these things to perfection because I have not. But I am saying I know the way to Santa Fe.

Here we go. Drum roll please. We shall entitle it *The Eighteen Thoughts You Must Have to Stay In Business:*

- Make sure small business ownership is for you, or for you to continue in, what with its 70% failure rate and the general unpreparedness of OEs.

- Trouble (you?) is the first employee hired when you took on the OE gig. Expect it, reduce the amount you cause, and learn the methods of dealing with it. Keeping your ego out of decision making will reduce the trouble brought about from DWI.

- Yes, you are the leader so that means your employees find you out front, working 'A' tasks, treating everyone differently. Making sure you are bringing it with you when you are 'bringing it'. Know things you are supposed to know.

- Get your price MO (motus operandi in police talk) right. There is no such thing as a fair price. Banish the word 'free'. Raise prices some.

- Sell only products that eat and drink. B2B business is safer than retail business (B2C).

- Let your number one numerical focus be on the gross profit you generate, not sales dollars. This number is much more telling than revenue.

- Design your business for *sustainability.* This is the most important goal if you do not want to become a statistic. Focus on a business model that brings you this such as contract customers and eating and drinking products.

- Design for a broad base of customers—in the hundreds or thousands—that are under contract preferably. The broader the base the more stability you have. If your existence depends on a few large customers then you are already in trouble.

- Embrace salespeople and all the difficulties they present. Nothing happens until somebody sells something. Yes, they are difficult.

- Know how to fly the plane please, what to do when turbulence strikes, what the gauges are saying. Your instrument readings are your controls. Have an 'A' game.

- Cash is King and profit the Queen so please get this one right so that thy kingdom does come. AR is like people. It ages, turns delinquent, gets written off, and goes to court.

- Things are going to change! Count on it. Some changes may be strong enough to wipe you out. Others may be for the better. Beware the Change Monster!

- The Law of Negativity is a competitor to face down on a regular basis. For some reason, it takes five positive thoughts just to cancel out one negative one. One negative thought immediately attracts five others.

- Staying physically fit raises your business IQ 20 points over an OE who does not exercise. Spend at least two hours a week on it. Big return on this investment.

- Get tech but do not over automate the human factor. It serves you not the other way around. Apple has it right— There's an App for that!

- Have faith in the Law of the Pinball. Keep things in play, launch continuously, keep moving and you greatly increase your chances of solving your trouble as well as hitting pay dirt. Launch! Launch!

- Realize you and your company are your biggest competitors. But the good news-- who better to overcome you than you? Or is that the bad news? A lot to be gained here but not so much by worrying about your competitor.

- Yes, you can make it to the end zone! But the odds are against you. Either sell it or hand it over to keep vital passion in the business. You may need new TENEs along the way. Remember that one year in an OE's life is equal to one and a half years of a normal person's.

Well there it is. I have written about only things that can make a difference for you, especially correct thought. Plain talk, no diagrams or lengthy theories. I have been swayed by my experiences and the desire to help you avoid GOOB. I live where you are and should be able to speak about this place after abiding there 29 years. But I could still GOOB even if I state my 29 years a too often. I said to my VP this year that I will be happy when we make $5 YTD. That is, as a corporation, after everything. Like other businesses, e/Doc Systems is in the middle of the Great Recession and it is not much fun. We have seen sales drop 17% and have to take measures to keep in touch with a break even.

I know other business owners are suffering as well. I advise to deal with reality forthrightly. No illusions such as 'well the building we are buying is now worth (less than a billion dollars so we are good' or other blue sky denials. This period is the worst financial crises since 1929 and everyone is as serious as a car company asking for bailout money. As OE, you need to act accordingly meaning swiftly, honestly, quickly and do enough to assure at least a break even. No time for pride.

I end by giving my email TCIVLJ@aol.com and cell at 901-484-0105

Afterword
I have always got something to say

Like everyone, I continue to watch this economy eat jobs and destroy businesses. Some 2.6 million have lost their jobs in this economy, double the normal. The decline in real estate values seems to be at the heart of everything and it does not show signs of rising any time soon (see don't buy the building chapter). But if you are a buyer this is a great plus and a time to buy at a 20% discount. I think there will be many people, those who postponed buying in this economy, that will kick themselves years later and be saying to themselves "Man, I could have bought that thing for next to nothing but didn't."

The media loves to play up the huge indebtedness we are getting into as a country but, at the same time, has done a very poor job of explaining how at least the majority of that money should come back to the taxpayer. As written about, you would think a trillion dollars had just been given to drug addicts to buy more crack. Fact is, all those foreclosed homes that caused the crash still have significant value. They will be sold at some point for maybe 70 cents on the dollar allowing the citizens to recover about 700 billion of the trillion. The banks and companies that you and I bought at cents on the dollar would need to rise in value about 30% in the coming years for the money spent on them to come back. So a lot of the money is coming back at some point and then we can pay off China.

As business people we know there are two sides of the ledger, debit and credit, and such is the case here. There is a large debt, yes, but there are assets on the other side of the ledger. Troubled ones, sure. Totally worthless, no. Looking at that should make everyone feel a lot better than they do now and that alone would help the economy. It seems we only get the debit side of things presented by the news media and can only see five minutes into the future max.

Thrift is the keyword these days but if everyone is so scared that all they feel right about buying is toothpaste we will only stay in this thing longer. Consumers can still be conservative. If you need a new car and can keep the same payment step out and buy one. You may have been thinking of moving up to a larger home but instead decided to delay putting a For Sale sign in the yard. While it is true enough you will get about 20% less for your home than a year or two ago that will be offset by the fact you will pay the same 20% less for the new home so you should step out. As long as the U.S. population grows each year demand for new housing is built in. Plus, land is no longer being made. Don't forget that if you are a first time home buyer the government is giving you $8,000 in tax credit and you can file for it as soon as you close on the house.

This recession seems to have that Roosevelt thing of 'the only thing we have to fear is fear itself.' My business is off about 10% from last year but it is nothing I can't compensate for and I have done so. I am glad that I am not in the retail sector though. There is true bloodshed there.

It could be a good time to go into business by either buying one or starting one. I think this is especially so for strong executive type or sales type people who have lost jobs. Many non-compete agreements are not valid if one is fired so if this is you, you can go right back to your customers. Surely there is a lot of exceptional talent on the street looking right now so it is a good time for your business to find better expertise if it has been needing it.

I cannot picture anyone wanting to open a new restaurant or retail shop. If you knew how to interpret the stimulus package you could set up in a business that is going to benefit from it. Seek companies to apply to that are going to benefit from it. Most state and local governments are going to benefit so there may be some job openings there that would not be ordinarily. It could be a good time to go back to a school and increase your marketability.

It seems we are in for at least another four years of the two political parties shouting at each other and trying to trip up the other. The constant denigrating of our presidents Nixon, Clinton, Bush, by comedians and media, has hurt us all. The president is our leader and if he is bashed then so are we and our country. Imagine yourself, as leader of your company, if you were degraded most of the time. The business may just slowly go away. Maybe this is what our country is doing. I hope not. There are so many good people in this country but they just do not seem to make it to elective office. Small businesses, as the country's largest employer, can only suffer from all this crap.

The recession may serve to wring excess out of our system. America is a wasteful, throwaway type society both at home and business. Just making good use of what we already have or repairing it, could bring us the economic savings we are looking for. It is amazing what you can do around your own house by re-using things, putting on a sweater instead of the heat, growing stuff in a garden, buying second hand or selling off some of your excess stuff. I think a business that helped people do this could do well. Maybe they could bring back the MacGyver show We could learn again from him how to make the most of anything. Make him a Cabinet member.

Speaking of such, shouldn't there be The Secretary of Saving Money in the President's lineup? And the Secretary of Small Business since we employ the most people and endure the most trouble?

Encouraging your kids to join the Scouts might be smart prep for the future. Kids don't need to get lost on how to do practical stuff in their Twitter, Facebook, texting and computer world. But as small business owners we should be right at home with all this adversity and change. It is our stock in trade isn't it? We know how to do this. If not, read this book again.

Since you are reading this I dearly thank you for buying the book. It has been a thrill to write and have someone publish it. Thank you Morgan James Publishing of New York, my publisher. I always have something to say so what a great outlet. It has given me new rocket fuel to burn and I hunt that in my semi-retired world. See the Law of the Pinball at work here because I have stayed in motion. Then I hit on this book! Using it as a base I can give seminars, consult some and even go on book tours. Just do it as I like to do it. One thing leading to another as I wrote about. Maybe I will write another one. I've always got something to say.

ABOUT THE AUTHOR

TOM PEASE has owned an office equipment dealership called e/Doc Systems Inc. in Memphis, TN., for the past 29 years and counting. Other business ownership positions have included a full line Kawasaki dealership as well as a document shop. He is an accredited small business consultant.

Tom, 59, graduated from the University of Tennessee Knoxville with a B.S. in Communications. His next stop was two years in the Navy aboard the USS Newport 1179. He worked for IBM six years winning local and national sales awards. In 1981 he and two others formed the business he still operates.

In 1994 he won the *Memphis Business Journal's* Small Business Executive of the Year.

He is a member of St. Ann Catholic church and founded the Kenny Dolan Memorial Scholarship Fund there now in its 14th year.

Tom and his wife Cindy have been married 34 years. They have two children, Parker and Lacey. Their home is on 70 acres of land with dogs Pete and Sam, Dusty the family donkey, Chief a paint horse, Woody the beaver and other assorted wildlife. Among his prized possessions are his Caterpillar bulldozer and Kubota tractor.

This is his first book.

Visit www.tompeaseconsulting.com

The Family and the Foundation

Left to right: Cindy McLarty, V.P. 20+ yrs., Linda Camp, Sales rep, 20+ yrs., Parker Pease, Sales Manager, Lacey Pease, daughter, Cindy Pease, Secretary and wife, Theo Harris, Service Manager, 20+ yrs., Mark Stevens, Technician, 20+ yrs.

BONUS PAGE
Two Free Hours For Your Business With
TP Business Coaching

As you have read in *Going Out of Business By Design* and probably experienced for yourself, there are many potholes and pressure cookers that entrepreneurs endure. Possibly you could use some help! That is the purpose of Tom Pease Consulting. There is always something that can be done and my best skill is creatively solving difficult problems.

I am accredited by the Institute for Independent Business as a Small Business Coaching but more importantly have the experience bank of doing what you are doing for the past 29 years.

My program is pretty simple. There are no long term contracts or expensive programs. I have a billable service of $100 an hour for phone support or on site. There is a monthly program of $1000 or $2,000.

I can perform the financial and operational analysis that most consultants do. In all honesty, I think the best help comes from a well experienced peer that you can discuss confidential matters with frankly and get feedback. CEO's notoriously keep many matters to themselves but a consultant can be a valuable sort of temporary co-CEO.

901-484-0105

BUY A SHARE OF THE FUTURE IN YOUR COMMUNITY

These certificates make great holiday, graduation and birthday gifts that can be personalized with the recipient's name. The cost of one S.H.A.R.E. or one square foot is $54.17. The personalized certificate is suitable for framing and will state the number of shares purchased and the amount of each share, as well as the recipient's name. The home that you participate in "building" will last for many years and will continue to grow in value.

Here is a sample SHARE certificate:

HABITAT FOR HUMANITY

THIS CERTIFIES THAT
YOUR NAME HERE
HAS INVESTED IN A HOME FOR A DESERVING FAMILY

1985-2005
TWENTY YEARS OF BUILDING FUTURES IN OUR
COMMUNITY ONE HOME AT A TIME

1200 SQUARE FOOT HOUSE @ $65,000 = $54.17 PER SQUARE FOOT
This certificate represents a tax deductible donation. It has no cash value.

YES, I WOULD LIKE TO HELP!

I support the work that Habitat for Humanity does and I want to be part of the excitement! As a donor, I will receive periodic updates on your construction activities but, more importantly, I know my gift will help a family in our community realize the dream of homeownership. **I would like to SHARE in your efforts against substandard housing in my community!** *(Please print below)*

PLEASE SEND ME _____ SHARES at $54.17 EACH = $ $_____

In Honor Of: _____

Occasion: (Circle One)   HOLIDAY   BIRTHDAY   ANNIVERSARY

       OTHER: _____

Address of Recipient: _____

Gift From: _____ *Donor Address:* _____

Donor Email: _____

I AM ENCLOSING A CHECK FOR $ $_____ PAYABLE TO HABITAT FOR HUMANITY OR PLEASE CHARGE MY VISA OR MASTERCARD *(CIRCLE ONE)*

Card Number _____ Expiration Date: _____

Name as it appears on Credit Card _____ Charge Amount $ _____

Signature _____

Billing Address _____

Telephone # Day _____ Eve _____

PLEASE NOTE: Your contribution is tax-deductible to the fullest extent allowed by law.
Habitat for Humanity • P.O. Box 1443 • Newport News, VA 23601 • 757-596-5553
www.HelpHabitatforHumanity.org